MBAPPÉ

LUCA CAIOLI
&
CYRIL COLLOT

ICON

Published in the UK in 2018
by Icon Books Ltd, Omnibus Business Centre,
39–41 North Road, London N7 9DP
email: info@iconbooks.com
www.iconbooks.com

Sold in the UK, Europe and Asia
by Faber & Faber Ltd, Bloomsbury House,
74–77 Great Russell Street, London WC1B 3DA or their agents

Distributed in the UK, Europe and Asia
by Grantham Book Services,
Trent Road, Grantham NG31 7XQ

Distributed in Australia and New Zealand
by Allen & Unwin Pty Ltd,
PO Box 8500, 83 Alexander Street,
Crows Nest, NSW 2065

Distributed in South Africa
by Jonathan Ball, Office B4, The District,
41 Sir Lowry Road, Woodstock 7925

Distributed in India by Penguin Books India,
7th Floor, Infinity Tower – C, DLF Cyber City,
Gurgaon 122002, Haryana

Distributed in Canada by Publishers Group Canada,
76 Stafford Street, Unit 300, Toronto, Ontario M6J 2S1

Distributed in the USA
by Publishers Group West,
1700 Fourth Street, Berkeley, CA 94710

ISBN: 978-1-78578-418-7

Typeset in New Baskerville by Marie Doherty

Printed and bound in Great Britain by Clays Ltd, Elcograf S.p.A.

MBAPPÉ

About the authors

Luca Caioli is the bestselling author of *Messi, Ronaldo* and *Neymar*. A renowned Italian sports journalist, he lives in Spain.

Cyril Collot is a French sports journalist. He is the author of several books and documentaries about French football, and the bestselling biographies *Griezmann, Pogba* and *Martial.*

Contents

Chapter 1

Allée des Lilas

He was told about the visit beforehand and has prepared diligently. He's written down some thoughts in blue pen. He can't wait to read them out, but his grandmother tells him to wait, he'll be able to do it later. Now is not the time: his grandparents and their guests are chatting and drinking coffee. He looks back at the notebook he has put on the table of the small living room dominated by a large television, listening and sometimes intervening in the conversation. He is finally given permission, which comes with a recommendation: read loudly and pronounce the words clearly.

'Hello everyone, Kylian is the best. He is the hero of Bondy. Everyone loves him. He's a role model for all children who play football. He is very good. Wilfrid and Fayza have raised their children well. Ethan will follow in the footsteps of his brother, Kylian.'

Idrisse is nine years old; he goes to school, plays football in the Under 10s and, with a handful of words, summarises what everyone in Bondy thinks, from Madame la Maire to the kids who train on the pitches of the Stade Léo-Lagrange just a few hundred metres away.

Idrisse is the grandson of Elmire and Pierrot Ricles, a couple who came to France from Martinique in the late 1970s. They live on the first floor of a white building at number 4, Allée des Lilas. A five-storey 1950s council building in a quiet tree-lined street in the centre of Bondy, an area that some pompously call the Cité de Fleurs thanks to the names of its streets. It was here that – in the autumn of 1998 – the Mbappé family came to live. As you climb the first flight of stairs, there is a post box that still says Lamari-Mbappé Lottin 2nd Left.

'They moved in on the floor right above us,' says Elmire, 'into an apartment identical to ours: 56 square metres, living room, a kitchenette with a view of the Stade Léo-Lagrange, and two bedrooms. I remember that when they arrived Fayza was in the last months of her pregnancy with Kylian.'

Fayza – 24 years old at the time and originally from Algeria – grew up in Bondy Nord, in the Terre Saint Blaise neighbourhood. She attended the Collège Jean Zay and went to the gym right across from the house. She played basketball when she was twelve and thirteen, before focusing on handball. She played on the right wing for AS Bondy in Division 1.

'She started at the bottom and became one of Bondy's best handball players in the late 1990s. Fayza had charisma. She was one of the leaders of the team, super talented and super tough,' remembers a family friend.

'She was a fighter on the court but she was also hot-headed. It didn't take much to wind her up and she wasn't always friendly to the opposition. If you crossed Fayza, you remembered it,' recalled Jean-Louis Kimmoun, a former director and president of the club in an interview with *Le Parisien*. 'But off the pitch, she was, and still is a very sweet person.'

'She likes to talk a lot though. She used to play pranks all the time. I worked with her for three or four years as an instructor in the Maurice Petitjean and Blanqui neighbourhoods, on Wednesdays and during the school holidays in the community centres. That was where she met Wilfrid, also an instructor, with his little brother Pierre and Alain Mboma, big brother of Patrick Mboma, African Footballer of the Year in 2000. They both loved sport, liked taking the mickey and had strong characters. They were bound to be attracted to each other,' explains a friend of the couple.

When he moved into Allée des Lilas with Fayza, Wilfrid was 30; he was born in Douala in Cameroon and had come to France in search of a better life. After living in Bobigny, he moved to Bondy Nord, where he played football for years.

'He was a good player, a number 10, a midfielder who was fond of keeping the ball,' according to Jean-François Suner, AS Bondy technical director, known to everyone as Fanfan. 'He could have had a career. He rose through the ranks at the club then played for two years in the Division d'Honneur for the neighbouring club [Bobigny]. When he stopped, he came back to us. We offered him a position and he devoted himself to our young players as an instructor, then as sporting director. We worked together for almost 30 years, from the 1988–9 season, and we restructured the club. He left in June 2017.'

20 December 1998

It had been five months and a handful of days since that famous 'One, two, three nil!' Since the two headed blows inflicted by Zinedine Zidane and the *coup de grâce* from Emmanuel Petit in the final of the World Cup, knocking out the Brazil of Ronaldo, the ailing phenomenon. The memory of that Sunday 12 July and the collective delirium was still fresh. How could you forget one and a half million people celebrating, intoxicated with joy, on the Champs Élysées, singing victory songs?

'*Black-blanc-beur*' (Black-White-North African), with the crowd chanting 'Zizou for President!' How could you forget one of the greatest achievements in the history of French sport? It was fitting that in that year blessed by football Fayza and Wilfrid should have received the best Christmas present of all: their first child. He was born on 20 December and was christened with the name Kylian Sanmi (short for Adesanmi,

meaning 'the crown fits me' in Yoruba) Mbappé
Lottin. Mbappé, a surname that would give rise to a
thousand assumptions: was Kylian the grandson of
Samuel Mbappé Léppé, nicknamed 'Le Maréchal', the
Cameroonian midfielder of the 1950s and 60s? Or a
relative of Étienne M'Bappé the bassist from Douala?
No, there was no connection, as Pierre Mbappé would
explain: in Cameroon, the surname Mbappé is as common as Dupont in France or Martin in the UK.

Pierre is Kylian's uncle, a footballer who trained with
Stade de l'Est before joining clubs such as Levallois,
Villemomble and Ivry.

He dashed to the hospital to meet his nephew, taking the newborn a mini football as a gift. Joking with
Fayza and his brother Wilfrid, he said: 'You'll see, he'll
be a great footballer one day!'

A few days after the happy event, mother and son
came home. Fayza returned to work at the Mairie de
Bobigny while Wilfrid only needed to cross the road to
get to the football pitches at the Stade Léo-Lagrange to
train his kids. There was one in particular that attracted
his attention: he was eleven years old and had come to
Bondy five years earlier from Kinshasa, then in Zaire,
now in the Democratic Republic of the Congo. The
situation was difficult in his country so his parents
had decided to send him to France to give him the
chance to study and build himself a future. The boy
was called Jirès Kembo-Ekoko; he was the son of Jean

Kembo, known as 'Monsieur But' (Mr Goal), a mid-fielder for the Zaire team that twice won the Africa Cup of Nations (1968 and 1974), who also scored two goals against Morocco in 1973, helping his team become the first team from sub-Saharan Africa to qualify for the World Cup (Germany 1974). Jean called his son Jirès in honour of Alain Giresse, the French midfielder he admired so much, and sent him to France to live with an uncle and his older sister. In 1999, Jirès Kembo-Ekoko received his first player registration at AS Bondy. Wilfrid was his first coach and soon also became his legal guardian and father.

'It's hard to explain but it was instinct, as if that person had always been my destiny,' Jirès would say years later. The Lamari-Mbappé Lottin family took him into their home; they did not adopt him but he would always call them Mum and Dad because they were the ones who gave him affection, helped him overcome a difficult social situation and realise his dream of becoming a professional footballer. Jirès went to live in Allée des Lilas and became little Kylian's big brother, role model, idol and first footballing hero. The neighbours remember when he would come home for the weekend from the INF Clairefontaine Academy, or when Fayza and Wilfrid would take him to important matches.

'They were a very close family, nice down-to-earth people,' says Pierrot.

'We didn't see Wilfrid much because of his work

but we would bump into Fayza a lot on the stairs or in the local shops. We saw Kylian grow up. As soon as he started walking, he started kicking a ball around in the room upstairs from my two girls. On Sunday mornings, I think he turned his room into a football pitch!' Elmire remembers with a laugh.

'Whenever I saw her, Fayza never stopped apologising. I told her it was fine and that you can hardly tie a child up! Even then, you could see his head was full of football.'

Another laugh and the grandmother talks about the time when they gave the little boy upstairs a *djembe* drum one Christmas or birthday. 'He never stopped, it took him a while to forget his new toy. But apart from the football and the drum, Kylian was a lovely, very polite boy who would always say '*Bonjour*' or '*Bonsoir*' whenever he saw me. We didn't get to watch him evolve as a footballer because a few years after the birth of Ethan, the baby of the family who, if my memory serves me correctly, came into the world in 2006, they moved to a residential neighbourhood in the south of the town, on the other side of the station, towards Les Coquetiers. We saw him in May last year when he came back to the stadium here to celebrate winning the French title. All the kids from AS Bondy were there, with a banner that said: "Thank you Kylian, everyone in Bondy is behind you!" It was really nice. Kylian gave the kids shirts and Idrisse even managed to get a picture with him.'

'Luckily Fayza saw us and shouted: "Wait, wait, that's my neighbour!" so I got into the van and took the photo that my Mum looks after now,' the grandson explains.

'We wrote a letter for the occasion, with the three other families that live here, with Daniel and Claudine Desramé, our neighbours on the first floor.'

Elmire gets up from the table, walks over to a corner of the room, opens a drawer and flicks through a mountain of paper. Eventually she exclaims: 'Here it is!'

Dear Kylian,

We hope you won't be shocked if we address you informally. We still remember you as the very well-brought up ten-year-old boy we would meet on the stairs of number 4, Allée des Lilas. Now, you're a big football star and you shine on the pitch. We're following the dazzling success of your sporting career with joy. We often talk about you and your parents we were so fond of. They gave you a very good education. Every time you lace up your boots, don't forget that your neighbours are your biggest fans!

With warm wishes for the future.

Chapter 2

The town where anothing is possible

You can't miss it. It's right in front of you as you go over the A3 towards Paris. It's huge. It occupies four floors of the side of the eight-storey Résidence des Potagers. It's an explosion of green, of leaves, of footballs spurting out everywhere. In the middle, looking serious and giving a 'shaka' sign, stands Kylian Mbappé, wearing a Paris Saint-Germain shirt. There's a slogan at the top: 'Bondy: the town where anything is possible.' It's a mega fresco that looks down from on high over a motorway that spews cars and traffic jams; it keeps an eye on Avenue du Général Galliéni (formerly the RN3), on the comings and goings of new businesses (from Conforama to Darty), and accompanies the kids that cross the street to go into the Lycée Madeleine-Vionnet and the groups of teenagers approaching the Collège Jean-Renoir. It is an honour, the kind of mural usually reserved for people like Zinedine Zidane, who, after the World Cup win in 1998, was entitled to a giant portrait on Marseille's Place Paul Ricard, looking out towards the Mediterranean. Like Diego Armando Maradona, immortalised by Jorit Agoch on a building in San Giovanni a Teduccio (Naples) or the giant poster of Moussa Sissoko on the façade of Le Galion in Aulnay.

The huge panel with the effigy of the PSG number 29 was paid for by Nike, who have been sponsoring the young centre forward since he was thirteen years old. The American sportswear brand has also put its hand into its pockets to build a community sports facility: it was opened on 6 September 2017, in the Jardin Pasteur, where Kylian learned to dribble for the first time and scored his first goals. Two symbols, the fresco and the sports facility, asked for by the Mbappé family as a tribute to the town where Kylian was born.

Bondy, in the Seine-Saint-Denis (93) *département* and the Île-de-France region, is a suburb to the north-east of Paris, nine kilometres from the city's Porte de Pantin. It is the ninth largest town in the *département*, a cosmopolitan municipality of almost 54,000 inhabitants, not counting the Canal de l'Ourcq area.

The name Bondy appears for the first time between 590 and 630 in the will of Ermenthrude, a rich widow who bequeathed land, an ox-cart, clothing and various objects of worship to the church built at the intersection of the ancient Roman Rue Compoise and the road from Lutetia to Meaux. There are two theories about the origin of the town's name: that it comes from Bonitius (in Latin, the son of Bonit), the owner of the land during the Gallo-Roman period, or that it is derived from the Gallic word 'bon', meaning 'hillock'. Over time, the name became Boniaticus, Boniasensis, Bonisiacus, Boniaticus (8th century), Bulzeia, Bonzeia (12th century), Bondis, and finally Bondy (17th century). It was during the 17th and 18th centuries that the name Bondy first became linked to the forest, the Bois de Bondy, well known at that time as a refuge for bandits. It was at the local post office where, in the night between 20 and 21 June 1791, Pierre-Augustin Fremin, a postmaster and future mayor, recognised Louis XVI fleeing from the Tuileries Palace disguised as a *valet de chambre*. His escape was short lived: the king of France was later arrested in Varennes. Today, all that is left of the famous forest is a few hectares to the extreme north of the *département*, but the town's coat of arms and its motto, 'Happy under its shade', still recall it.

In the late 18th century, Bondy had 300–400 inhabitants, who worked the land. It was from 1821 – with the end of the construction of the Canal de l'Ourcq by Napoleon to bring water to the capital – that the town experienced a period of great industrial and urban expansion, with the arrival of the territory's first mills and cement factories. Some claim these ended up here not only because of the land and water but because of the prevailing north-easterly winds taking smoke and fumes towards the provinces and far from the delicate nostrils of the capital's bourgeoisie. Between 1860 and

1870, with the arrival of the railway linking Paris to Strasbourg, many natives of Alsace and Lorraine who worked on the construction of the line moved into the area around the station. In the early 20th century, residential neighbourhoods developed to the south of the town: stone houses and a manor, typical of the Paris region. To the north, peasants still cultivated vegetables but everything changed with the advent of the new century. The automobile industry was booming; workers went to live near the factories and Bondy, like other parts of the Seine-Saint-Denis *département*, became a working-class city.

The class element is a significant one, given that a right-wing mayor has not been elected to the Town Hall since 1919. The town's mayors (with the exception of Henri Varagnat, a Communist Party mayor from 1935 to 1939, who, like all Communist elected officials, was removed at the outbreak of the Second World War) have always come from the ranks of the Socialist Party. Sylvine Thomassin is no exception. She came to Seine-Saint-Denis as a child, worked as a midwife in the maternity unit at the Jean Verdier hospital and then took over policies on education and urban renewal before becoming mayor in October 2011. She replaced Gilbert Roger, who had been elected to the post of senator. She considers the recent past, present and future of the town: 'From the 1950s and 60s, with the arrival of returnees from Algeria, immigrants from

North Africa, sub-Saharan Africa and Portugal, new neighbourhoods and large housing complexes were built in the north of the town to deal with the housing crisis and the dismantling of the slums. Bondy went from 22,411 inhabitants in 1954 to 51,653 in 1968. It was the first wave of migration,' explains Thomassin.

'It would be followed by a second, between 1980 and 1990, generally from countries south of the Sahara: Zaire, Cameroon, Congo and Angola. The housing estates allowed thousands of families to have access to hygienic conditions, drinking water and electricity. In short, to modern comforts. The right to housing was guaranteed; working-classes and middle-classes lived together happily. There was a strong and active community fabric in the neighbourhoods: it was the golden age. The estates worked well until the brutal rise in unemployment between 1970 and 1980. Then, little by little, those who went to live there did so through lack of any other option. The estates were designed to last for 30 years, but it's been twice as long now and enough is enough. We don't want any more to be built. It's a situation we're trying to change with the urban renewal project (PRU) launched in 2006 and now in its second phase.'

Bondy is a town under construction, or rather under reconstruction. To understand what this means, you only need to stroll down Rue Jules Guesde to Place du 11 Novembre 1918. Right in front of the Town Hall – a

building that is part Soviet, part functionalist in style –
there once stood a huge housing estate that stretched
as far as the RN3. The square is now home to pleas-
ant, well-looked after buildings in a range of colours,
from white to wood; they do not exceed five stories
and boast the windows of new shops and businesses
on the ground floor. It is a piece of urban planning
that is profoundly changing the fabric of the town, its
services, green spaces, infrastructure and housing policy. Not limited to the centre, it runs to five neighbourhoods, including those to the north considered the
most problematic.

'We want to change the face of the city, recreate a
place, an open space where people want to live, to live
together,' adds the mayor.

It is not the only ambitious project: urban renewal
also involves a new economic model and a profound
change in the industrial fabric.

'Starting with the crisis in the oil industry, we've seen
a process of de-industrialisation. Many factories have
been relocated to other regions or other countries.
Now the Seine-Saint-Denis *département* is gambling on
attracting other types of businesses. But it's not easy,
especially because the state has made other choices,
favouring Paris and the west of the capital,' continues
the mayor.

'But we're not feeling sorry for ourselves, we've
rolled up our sleeves and started working. Bond'innov,

the first business incubator, came into being in 2011. It now plays host to and supports about 40 innovative entrepreneurs who want to develop their projects in the fields of life sciences and biotechnology, in particular digital technologies; the environment; the social and solidarity economies; north–south relations; cooperation and international development focused on Africa.'

Sylvine Thomassin stresses: 'We're trying to build a solid and close-knit town capable of integrating into the dynamics of the Grand Paris region.'

That may be true, but what does Bondy, the town where anything is possible, have to do with the image of Kylian Mbappé?

'"The town where anything is possible" is a slogan launched long before the phenomenal rise of Kylian. It didn't come from sport but from education and culture, two themes that, little by little, are becoming part of Bondy's DNA,' explains the Socialist official.

'First and foremost, the Maîtrise de Radio France choir school. Founded in 1946, in Paris, it was one of the few institutions that tried to address the issue of what could be done for the *banlieues* after the riots in 2005. Eleven years ago, it decided to open a second headquarters here, with the aim of giving kids from the north the opportunity to discover music, learn about it and play it to a high level. That same year, 2005, also saw the birth of the Bondy Blog, which tells the story of diversity in France, and, since 2009, we have had a satellite of the École Supérieure de Journalisme de Lille that allows kids who can't count on their parents' wallets when it comes to enrolling in important universities to learn the craft of journalism. We founded the "cafés philos" and the Université Populaire Averroès, in which 1,900 people have registered. Who would ever have thought that in a working-class town like Bondy there were so many people interested in courses about mathematical problems, art history, music through the centuries and astronomy? That some 1,900 people attend the university, not to graduate, but for the pleasure of learning, is really wonderful.

'And there's another factor that makes us very proud, our success rate at *baccalauréat* level: 87 per cent in a town that, in terms of socio-professional categories for national education, would not be expected to exceed 73 per cent. Not only that but ten to fifteen years ago, when kids from Bondy passed the *bac*, the most they would choose would be a BTS [technical higher education diploma]. They would self-censor, believing they wouldn't be able to continue their studies, but today, thanks to teacher volunteering and priority education agreements with institutes such as Sciences Po and the University Pierre and Marie Curie, they know that success is possible for them too, that you can do it in the *banlieue* just like you can do it anywhere else, just like in the top Parisian high schools.'

And Kylian Mbappé is living proof of this success?

'Kylian is the pride of the town. We're hugely proud that we've given the metropolis of Grand Paris and the whole of France such a wonderfully talented young man who has even instilled a passion for football in people like me who prefer rugby! He's a boy who hasn't forgotten Bondy. He is an ambassador for the region and living proof that this really is the town where anything is possible.'

'He's leading the charge,' adds Oswald Binazon, equipment manager at the stadium. 'But we've got so many athletes who've reached the top in handball, rugby, fencing, judo and football. We also have teams like AS Bondy in men's basketball, who won the French title in National 1 in 1998, while the women's handball team reached Division 1. Bondy is a sport-mad town, thanks in part to a political will to get children playing sport. The former mayor, Claude Furzier, founded the Bondy Sporting Association in 1978, which now includes 26 disciplines and has 3,700 members. AS Bondy goes into schools to get young people involved in sport. There are handball and basketball courts in the playgrounds. We have a tennis complex, two swimming pools, five gyms and five community multi-sport facilities in the town, including the one opened by Nike in the Jardin Pasteur. Where's the heart of sport in Bondy? Here, at the Léo-Lagrange sports complex.'

Chapter 3

Oulala, Oulala

By six in the evening all the pancakes have disappeared. Like every Wednesday, training day, and every Saturday, match day, Karima makes more than a hundred. There's no trace of them now. The little footballers, hungry and greedy, have to return to the pitches of the Stade Léo-Lagrange disconsolate, without a steaming plate and a Nutella moustache. The most they can buy is a drink or a few sweets. But it's not the same. Next to the snack bar, Athmane Airouche smiles as he sips a nice coffee made by Karima. There's no shortage of that. He greets the boys who come to say hello and shake his hand before going into the dressing room. He then goes to check on the work of the Under 11 instructor.

Since June 2017, Airouche has been the president of AS Bondy, after being both a player and instructor in the Under 19 category, a 'rebellious age', he confesses. With his back to the scribbled green graffiti of the club's name and the word 'football', he reels off some facts and figures: 'We have 800 members, ranging from Under 7s to seniors. There are 140 girls, almost double compared to last season. Is it the Kylian effect?

Yes, it seems that way, and unfortunately we've had to turn down so many boys. We don't have the facilities or the capacity to take them. There are two football pitches here, one artificial, one grass, an indoor futsal hall and the Stade Robert-Gazzi on the other side of Bondy. We're a training club, we know how to work with kids and young people and that's our mission. We've never thought about taking on anything else. Although it should be pointed out that we've trained more than 30 boys who've gone on to turn professional. Last season, four of our students ended up at PSG, Bordeaux and Monaco.

Ours is a family club that plays a social role. We don't pick children based on their technique or skills, we take them because we want them to do some sport, play and have fun. We see no difference between those who come from Bondy North or Bondy South, from a middle-class or working-class family. From the moment they come through the stadium gates they're all budding footballers as far as we're concerned. We also keep an eye on their schooling and meet their teachers and families. We try to pass on values such as education, respect for others and rules, work that is serious and done well. And we insist on the importance of study; not everyone can become a big football star. It's a shame that sometimes the parents put the pressure on.

They're obsessed with the idea of having a son who's a footballer. Just the other day I had a long discussion with a father. In the end I asked him: "But wouldn't you be happy if your son became a good lawyer?"'

What about Kylian Mbappé?

'We often talk about him because a player with his qualities comes through perhaps only every 30 to 40 years in the life of a club like ours. We use him as an example to the kids for the attitude he has on and off the pitch. Everyone here is proud of Kylian. Why? Because he was born in this club and stayed here for nine years.'

Karima interrupts the president. Someone is looking for him. He leaves for a few minutes then comes back, ready to chat again.

'He lived over there,' says Airouche, gesturing with a wave of his hand beyond the stadium walls to the white buildings of Allée des Lilas. 'This was his kindergarten,' adds the president. 'He was here every day, always with his father, who was the technical director for the categories from U11 to U17. Kylian must have been three or four years old. He was the club's little mascot. You would see him come into the dressing room holding a ball and sit in the corner, in silence, to hear what the manager had to say before the game. I don't think there can be any other kids in the world who've listened to so many conversations. There can't be many who've heard so many technical discussions, tactics, sermons and lectures. And because Kylian has always been a sponge, someone who learns very quickly, from an early age he assimilated football concepts that others only heard and understood years later.'

When he was three and four, the little mascot would joke around with his father because he wanted to be enrolled at AS Bondy. He wanted to play with the big boys. But Wilfrid thought it was too soon and was concerned that, as an instructor himself, he was too close to be able to coach him properly. The future genius of French football had to be content for the time being with kick-abouts with his peers on the mini pitch next to the École Maternelle Pasteur, where Fayza took him every morning. Sometimes, he would allow himself to amaze the grown-ups where his father worked.

'I trained the goalkeepers because I used to be one myself, while Wilfrid concentrated on strikers. We grouped together the U17s, U19s and seniors to make a single group,' remembers Fanfan, Jean-François Suner, who has just arrived at the stadium to oversee training.

'We ended with a drill in front of the goal and Kylian, who was five at the time, was determined to play. He shouted, "I want to play! I want to play!" and his father said, "Stop it, Kylian. You can see that you can't." After a while I said to his father, "Go on, Wil. Let him play." He started doing the drill. He was five! He started wellying the ball and we laughed! Of course, he was noticeably slower but he had a special quality, he could whip the ball in a way that was incredible. Even the keepers couldn't believe it. They said: "Who is this little guy?" I just kept repeating to myself "Oulala, Oulala".'

It was an expression everyone would say over and over again when, at aged six, Kylian would finally be allowed to enrol at AS Bondy. His first coach was his dad, a man Airouche would describe as: 'Generous, a hard-worker and fair. Like Fayza, his wife. I can only think of them together because they're like two halves of a whole. The good things they did for their children they also did for the kids from here. They never saw any difference. For example, Fayza would always say to me: "When I buy a house I want a big pitch so the little ones from the club can come and play football." Even now that they've moved to Paris, we're still in touch. Whenever I speak to them, they repeat a hundred times: "Athmane, if you need anything for the club, you know we're always here." They're unusually generous. And don't forget that all the kids at our club have Nike gear, thanks to Kylian.'

But what was Wilfrid like as a coach to his son?

'He didn't do him any favours. He wouldn't hesitate to make Kylian squirm if it was for his own good and to show there wasn't any favouritism. He was tough, but he was the same with the other kids. You felt that he was a true instructor and really loved being part of the club,' explains the father of one of the boys who played with Kylian. And what was PSG's future number 29 like?

'A child like all the others who dream of becoming footballers, only that he had qualities the others didn't,' adds Airouche.

'He did things that were harder than the others, better than the others and faster than the others. And he would do them in every game. He was ten, twenty, 100 times better than the others. It really was extraordinary.'

Antonio Riccardi, who has been at AS Bondy for twelve years, first as a player, now as head of the U15s, is categorical. He has just finished training and, in a small room in the dressing room with kids coming and going, he remembers when he started coaching Kylian. 'I've known him ever since he was a baby because Wilfrid is like a second father to me: he's the one who trained me as a player and a coach. I remember Kylian at four years old, singing the Marseillaise with his hand on his heart or when, at six or seven, he would tell you not to worry and that someday he would be playing for the national team in the World Cup.'

'It's true, he said it all the time at that age,' remembers another former teammate. 'He wanted to win the Ballon d'Or, turn pro and play for Real. We would tell him to shut up!'

'All you could do was smile, when he was seriously planning out his future: Clairefontaine, Rennes, like his brother Jirés Kembo, then the France team, Madrid. We just thought he was a dreamer,' claims Riccardi. But, on the pitch, the boy from Allée des Lilas showed he was much more than that.

Fanfan explains: 'I had him for a year when he was playing above his age category in the Under 10s. At training, you could see right away that he had a technical ease. We knew he would go right to the top if there weren't any physical glitches. He only did four months with us in the Under 7s, then he always played above his category with players born in 1997, and even in 1996. Because his birthday is at the end of the year, he was practically playing against opponents who were three years older than him.'

'And despite that, he was the best on the pitch,' adds Riccardi. 'He made the difference. Quickly, very quickly, like he was a senior playing at a high level, he understood how to shake off his marker, how to get free for his teammates. What was his best quality? His pace with the ball at his feet. He had innate gifts.'

'He's a born dribbler. He's one of those players who just have something, like Messi, Neymar or Dembélé. He's mature and he's never put pressure on himself. When I see him playing professionally I say to myself that he was exactly the same when he was with us,' confirms Suner.

Riccardi confesses: 'As a coach, you could only give him advice about making decisions on the pitch, such as that he should have shot earlier, he should have passed the ball, he should've dribbled past one more opponent, but otherwise there was nothing else to teach him. He was technically extraordinary and there was no need to repeat anything twice. He immediately understood what the coach was asking of him.'

Just outside the dressing room it is bitterly cold and pitch black. On the other side of the playing area, the stand and the graffiti on the boundary wall ('faster, higher, stronger', a motto that could almost be Kylian's) is now hard to make out. The floodlights only light up the boys and girls on the patchy green as they practise drills, passing and shots on goal, over and over. In the warmth of the dressing room, the memories and anecdotes of AS Bondy's former player come full circle.

'His idol was Cristiano Ronaldo. He wallpapered his room with posters of the Portuguese player. He liked him when he was at Manchester United and during his first few years at Madrid, the fast number 7, up and down the wing. He liked his dribbling and would watch him on television and try to repeat it on the pitch,' remembers Riccardi. But the five-time Ballon d'Or winner was not the only star Kylian admired. There was also Ronaldinho and Zidane. His childhood friends still make fun of him for the time he showed up at the hairdressers and asked, in all seriousness, for the same style as Zizou. They looked at him as if he had gone mad. Years later, Kylian would try to justify it: 'When you like a player, you want to do everything just like them. Back then, I didn't know it was baldness!'

Mamadou Yate, technical coordinator of the U10 to U17 categories, is coaching late into the evening but has time to stop to chat to the visitors. 'I'd heard about Kylian from his father, who was an instructor in the town. He would come into schools to introduce the boys to football and he coached my friends. I'd heard he was very good, that the boy had skills, but when I met him for the first time he amazed me. It was 2005 and I was coaching a team in the same category at a nearby club, Stade de l'Est. We played a proper derby against Bondy. At the end of the first half, it was 0–0 and things were going well for us. But it didn't end that way: we lost 5–1, I think. Kylian must have scored three goals. Three incredible goals. He knew how to do things only the grown-ups could do. He could see the game before everyone else and when he had the ball at his feet my kids would stand back. They were afraid he would dribble past and make fools of them.'

A phenomenon on the pitch, less of a phenomenon at school. After the Pasteur nursery school, Kylian Mbappé attended the École Primaire Olympe de Gouges. In an interview with *L'Équipe* magazine, Yannick Saint-Aubert, the school's former headmaster, remembered that Fayza had an appointment with him and Marc, Kylian's teacher, every night to find out how her son's day had been. How he had behaved, whether he had done his exercises and what his grades had been. 'Kylian knew that if his grades were bad, Fayza and Wilfrid would not go easy on him. And he was smart enough to know exactly when he had to knuckle down.' Both mother and father followed the education and upbringing of their firstborn closely. They enrolled him in tennis lessons, swimming lessons and musical theatre, where he learned to play the flute. And to make sure he didn't fall in with a bad crowd, they ended up putting him in a private Catholic school in Bondy: the Groupe Scolaire Assomption. They watched over him there too. As Nicole Lefèvre, his French teacher remembers, he was the only pupil in Year 8 with a tracking sheet. Every hour, he had to have it signed by his teachers, who had to write down how he had behaved: well, very well or badly.

Intelligent; lively; mischievous; a dreamer; nice; hyperactive; unruly and difficult to manage: this is how some of his teachers describe him. The problem was not French, geography or maths – his results were often satisfactory – the problem was his behaviour, his way of doing things and his pranks. He was a boy who couldn't sit still at his desk to listen to his teacher's explanations, and, after a while, he would get bored. The slowness of the rhythm at school was not for him. Or, perhaps, simply, 'School was not his priority. Kylian had one idea in his head and that was becoming a professional footballer,' says François Suner.

'He loved football, thought about football and talked about football all the time, even when he wasn't here. He would play in the living room at home or sit in front of his PlayStation for a game of FIFA. And when there was a match on TV, you could be sure he wouldn't miss it. On top of all that, he grew up in a family where everyone loved football, his father and his uncle,' explains Riccardi.

Talent, passion, determination and family roots: a cocktail that made Kylian a little genius, popular with his coaches and teammates. 'Everyone was very impressed, both the players on our team and our opponents,' remembers Théo Suner, who played with Kylian in almost every category at AS Bondy and is now their U19 goalkeeper in D1. 'Whenever he got the ball, he would take out several players in one go. I remember an U11 tournament in Tremblay when he was amazing. We went a really long way, despite the fact that clubs like FC Porto and Feyenoord Rotterdam were playing. He carried the team throughout the competition. I've played with lots of footballers who have gone on to turn professional and I've never seen anything like that before, no one came close to his level. He was either dribbling past everyone, scoring or providing assists.'

'He was capable of scoring 50 goals a season in the U13s, in the lower categories. We didn't even count the goals. He could score three in one game and provide two assists. With me, he always played on the left wing. On the right wing was Jonathan Ikoné, who is now at Montpellier on loan to PSG. They had a good understanding, both on and off the pitch. Kylian was a good friend, he was fun and always smiling. He never had any problems with his teammates or with me. No, he wasn't the leader of the team like a captain who gives his teammates a hard time, but he became a leader on the pitch, he was the leader of a great team.'

In addition to the two already mentioned, the 1998–9 generation at AS Bondy also included Joé Kobo (now at Caen) and Metehan Güclü (now at PSG). But Kylian was the star of the team. 'I remember one league game, we were playing to stay up. We were ahead 2–0 but they pulled one back for 2–1. One of his team-mates told Kylian that they were bound to equalise now. He replied, telling him to calm down, wait and that he would score a goal in the next few minutes. So, Kylian picked up the ball in our half, dribbled past every-one, ended up in front of the opposition's goalkeeper, sent him one way with a feint and then scored with a Messi-esque lob. His father was on the bench with me and he wanted to kill him because he wasn't playing up to his level. When that happened, I said to him without thinking: "Don't kill him, go and congratulate him!"'

The memories keep on coming. François Suner adds another, perhaps one of the best about the lively little kid in a green and white shirt with the number 10 on his back. 'We were playing an important game against Bobigny. It was 0–0 at half-time and we were all over the place. It's true that in our teams we like to play with the ball, dictate the play and pass the ball around, but that day it wasn't working. At half-time, I went into the dressing room and asked the coach to let me say a few words. I spoke to the players and told them: "Listen, we're not going to get worked up today. It's simple, in the second half, we're just going to give the ball to Kylian. That's it." We won 4–0 and he was the one who scored the goals.'

One last question: did Kylian like pancakes with Nutella? 'Unfortunately, when he was playing the snack bar wasn't here,' explains Airouche. 'But now, whenever he comes to visit, he can make up for lost time.'

Chapter 4

The new attraction

Which scout in Île-de-France was the first to spot the player? It's hard to say; there are so many who claim to have discovered the future prodigy. There were soon dozens of recruiters. There was a large crowd on AS Bondy match days and some would have even been willing to pay to see the phenomenon in action.

It does seem, however, that Reda Hammache was one of the first representatives of a professional club to fall for Kylian. Aged 27, he was wearing two hats at the time, one as an instructor at the nearby club of US Saint-Denis and the other as a recruiter for the Paris region on behalf of Stade Rennais. It was this second role that took him to Bondy in February 2009. On the advice of a coach at the local club, he came to watch a game in the U13 league at the Stade Robert-Gazzi, US Bondy's other playing area in a picturesque location between the station and a working-class residential area. 'It was almost like a ground from another era!', jokes the former regional level defender, who has come a long way to become a member of the professional set-up at Lille in 2017, as well as the northern club's go-to expert on the French market. 'The pitch was as hard as cement that day but it didn't stop me from appreciating Kylian's talents. As he was playing two years above his age category, he was smaller and frailer than the others, but he already looked great and had a natural elegance. Whenever he touched the ball, something always happened. Even if not everything came off for him, I immediately saw that he was head and shoulders above the rest.'

They had already heard about the player in Rennes. On the pitches at the training academy, the kid had not gone unnoticed when he had come to the club since the recruitment of his older brother Jirès Kembo in 2004. So, when the first reports arrived, they were delighted to see what he could do.

In May 2009, the young winger was called up for a tournament in Giff-sur-Yvette, a small town in Essonne about twenty kilometres to the south-west of Paris. Stade Rennais use this opportunity every year to test out U12 players spotted in the Paris region. Although Kylian was a year younger, he was included in the team entrusted to Reda Hammache: 'We came seventh out of 32, which was a good result given how little our players knew each other. Kylian was very good, probably the best. It was a delight to see him play, although he tended to annoy his teammates by keeping the ball a bit too long sometimes.'

To get him to understand the importance of playing as a team and the need for defensive work, the young coach decided to move him to right-back for one game. 'He didn't stay in his position even for a second. He constantly came forward, never dropped back and did whatever he liked.' So as not to humiliate him and because Kylian had also made the difference going forward, Hammache left him on the pitch until the end of the match. But he did take the player to one side after the final whistle: 'I didn't want to irritate him, so I started by telling him everything he had done well. I also thanked him for helping us win the match. Then I moved onto the negative, to the fact that he hadn't followed the pre-game instructions. I made him understand that, as an instructor, I couldn't afford to pick a player who didn't listen to me. So he was going to be a substitute for the next game. He was angry, of course, but he understood my choice.'

The little pearl of Bondy began the following match on the bench, sulking and pouting until his team won a free-kick in a good position just outside the penalty area. His coach immediately asked to make a substitution: 'I called Kylian over and told him: "You're going on. This time I want you to play in an attacking position. Enjoy yourself, but first, take this free-kick for me." He ran off, took the time to place the ball, shot … and scored with a stunning strike! He was happy and rediscovered his smile and *joie de vivre* in an instant. He came to celebrate his goal with me by jumping into my arms. It sealed our friendship. After that, I could ask anything of him on the pitch and he would do it. I had gained his trust.'

The same was true of Kylian's parents, who appreciated the Rennais instructor's management style: 'At the end of the tournament, they came over to me and told me I was one of the few people to have understood how their son worked.' Despite these compliments and the positive experience at the Giff Cup, the Breton club did not manage to attract Kylian. 'He was still very young and it was very difficult for Rennes, as it was for other professional clubs, to bring him to their academies before he turned fifteen. And I don't think that the fact Jirès Kembo was with us was necessarily an advantage because he knew there were some difficulties in the first team at that time,' explains a former coach at the club.

After the Giff-sur-Yvette tournament, a video with some flattering comments began doing the rounds on social media: 'He's only ten years old but he's already being compared with the huge Man City star. There is a certain physical resemblance, but his technique in particular is strangely reminiscent of Robinho. There's still a long way to go, but lots of clubs already think he has what it takes to reach the highest level. What do you think?' wrote KEWJF as he posted his compilation on YouTube. Four minutes and twenty seconds featuring the kid, set to music. Whether he is wearing the green and white number 10 shirt of Bondy or the red number 6 shirt of Stade Rennais, Kylian provides plenty of material for the camera: a dribbling sequence followed by a little nutmeg, a subtle back-heel to get past an opponent, an impeccable Zidane-style Marseille turn and a free-kick into the top corner; his full technical repertoire is there for all to see. As a bonus, there is even a three-quarter shot of a celebration in which he makes the 'shaka' sign he would repeat some years later. This video, of course, contributed to maintaining the buzz around the phenomenon from Seine-Saint-Denis.

In the meantime, Reda Hammache had left Stade Rennais to join Racing Club de Lens, where he arrived during the 2009–10 season with two priorities: the midfielder Jeff Reine-Adélaïde, who would join the northern club before being picked up by Arsenal in 2015, and his other find, Kylian Mbappé. But the competition to get the player had become fierce: Paris Saint-Germain, Bordeaux and Caen were also lining up to get him to sign a non-solicitation agreement that would protect him from other French clubs until he could sign an apprentice contract at the age of fifteen.

For his parents, there was no question of getting carried away by this influx of offers. They wanted to take their time, discuss it, think about it and weigh up the pros and cons to make a sensible and group decision. 'Although Fayza and Wilfrid may seem open and charming at first, they are also very distrustful,' explains a close friend. 'They didn't want to rush it and felt they needed as much information as possible. Despite what some gossips may say, it was never a question of money for them, even if they did realise the sums that were at stake. Their approach was a correct one and they chose to turn to well-respected structures with a family feel, rather than leaning towards top clubs with more tempting financial offers.'

Stade Malherbe Caen – a modest French first division club that had its heyday in the 1990s by tasting the European Cup against the Spanish team Real Zaragoza – spotted Kylian in September 2009. 'He's a future Ballon d'Or winner,' was how David Lasry, the eyes of the Normandy club in the Paris region, described his latest find to his club directors. This obviously piqued the curiosity of Laurent Glaize, head of recruitment, who quickly took over the case and was not disappointed with a trip to Bondy: 'When I saw him play a month later, I immediately understood that we had a phenomenon on our hands. And I can tell you that I'd never used that word before. With our limited budgets, we had to move very quickly if we wanted to have a chance at getting Kylian.'

The staff at Caen made contact with the family. David Lasry came to see the player on several occasions and spoke with Wilfrid Mbappé about how the club did things. 'We didn't have Parisian means at our disposal and it wasn't in the club's policy to "buy" a kid. Our plans had a human element and were based on life at the club, making turning professional much easier in Caen than elsewhere. We knew it would be difficult but we decided to give it a go. We started out with little touches, like a Christmas present or a shirt for his birthday, and eventually made a low opening offer. When we didn't get a response, we decided to call the parents to check if they'd received our letter. And can you guess what Wilfrid's amused answer was? "There must be a page missing from your offer. You can't catch a shark with a fishing rod!" They weren't wrong, the kid already had quite a price on his head.'

Racing Club de Lens were also on the lookout. The arrival of Reda Hammache facilitated contact and the family eventually made the trip to Northern France in June 2010. They were welcomed by the director of training Marc Westerloppe, known in the field for having launched the career of Didier Drogba when he was at Le Mans. 'We spent the morning together, then Kylian took part in a match that afternoon with our U12s and some other trainees like him who were on trial. He was breath-taking during that game. I'd already had the chance to see him in action a month earlier at his club, but that day he did things I'd never seen from a boy of his age. His recruitment was a priority and I quickly informed my superiors.'

The following season, the candidates tried even harder to woo him. PSG offered to take Kylian to a tournament in Spain, but he chose instead to answer the call from Caen to play in the Jean-Pingeon Challenge, where he would be voted the player of the competition. Between September 2010 and June 2011, AS Monaco, FC Sochaux and the Girondins de Bordeaux, where Kylian had been seen several times at the 'Cap Girondins' camps, joined the discussions, as did Chelsea, the first big European club to take a position. In the spring of 2011, he was invited by the London club to spend a week at the Cobham training centre. It was a unique experience that would allow the little prodigy to discover a new mentality in the team then managed by Carlo Ancelotti, to meet Didier Drogba and especially to pull on a Blues shirt for a friendly won 7–0 against Charlton's U12s.

But Chelsea would not win the jackpot. The Mbappé clan did not follow up. 'It would have been too big an upheaval for the little one and his parents. And by then they had already narrowed it down to two,' confirms an insider. It came as no surprise that these were Racing Club de Lens and Stade Malherbe Caen. The month of May 2011 would be used to decide between them.

In the last stretch, Kylian's parents took more meetings. In Lens, they had several lunches with the president Gervais Martel and Marc Westerloppe, with whom they got on well. They did the same in Caen, where they asked to meet the first team manager Franck Dumas, the only person, or so they thought, who could guarantee Kylian's long-term footballing future. This interview would be decisive: 'Franck Dumas arrived late and hadn't eaten,' recalls an amused Laurent Glaize. 'He gulped down a sandwich, then asked to open the window of the meeting room that overlooked the training ground to light a cigarette. He sent his assistant to look after the players as it was the day before a decisive relegation game, but he trusted his staff and knew this was an important matter. The meeting lasted almost three hours and Franck Dumas was great! The atmosphere was relaxed and the coach, true to his reputation, was a riot of jokes and puns. He won the parents over with his friendliness and fatherly attitude. He explained to them that in Caen their little one wouldn't cut corners, that he would take good care of him and that as soon as he was ready, he would let him turn professional, without hesitation, just as he had done a month earlier with the young M'Baye Niang, who was sixteen.'

Fayza, Wilfrid and Kylian left Normandy delighted. A few weeks later, the verdict of the France Ligue 1 confirmed their mood. Caen stayed up with an encouraging fifteenth place finish, while the other 'finalists', Racing Club de Lens were relegated to Ligue 2 along with AS Monaco and Arles-Avignon. It was a matter of course: 'I will always remember when my phone rang,' says Laurent Glaize. 'I was on holiday, by the pool, when I saw Wilfrid's number flash up. He told me: "I'm telling you first, we've chosen Caen!" After two years of hard work on the case, the joy that we had pulled it off was immense!'

The offer would see Kylian join the training centre two years later, in August 2013, with a training-apprentice contract that would automatically lead to a professional deal. Caen would also have to pay a signing bonus set at €120,000 or €180,000 depending on the level of the first team at the time of Kylian's arrival. But for now, nothing had been signed, only their word had been given …

Chapter 5

And the winner is ...

Thierry Henry, Nicolas Anelka, William Gallas, Blaise Matuidi and Hatem Ben Arfa: they were all French internationals who had passed this way. Other players, such as Anthony Martial, would have loved to have been able to fine-tune their skills in the green heart of the Montjoye estate, about 50 kilometres to the south-west of Paris, but they had been turned down during the selection process. The National Football Institute in Clairefontaine-en-Yvelines, known commonly in France as the INF Clairefontaine, is not only the base camp for the French national team, but is also a sought-after place among young footballers from the Paris region. For the lucky and talented few, it has been possible since 1998 to enjoy optimal conditions almost free of charge for two years of pre-training between the ages of thirteen and fifteen, to prepare for entry into an academy at a professional club. 'The INF is a project with three dimensions: pastoral, sporting and educational,' explains its former director, Gérard Prêcheur, from his home. 'And although the primary objective for these kids may well be to achieve their dream, there's no question of them neglecting their studies or keeping the truth from them. The vast majority of them won't make it. In France, only 80 to 90 players manage to sign their first professional contract every year.'

What did this mean for Kylian? While waiting to join the Stade Malherbe Caen academy at fifteen, he entered the INF Clairefontaine in August 2011. A few months earlier, he had passed the selection tests with flying colours and impressed his audience. 'He quite simply stole the limelight,' remembers Prêcheur. 'I fell in love with the kid at first sight. On the ball, he combined technical skill with speed of execution, which is very rare at that age, and he also had this natural side to him that tried not to be conventional. He knew what he wanted: "To be a professional footballer", "to be one of the best", "to win the Ballon d'Or". It was already in his head and he expressed it very forcefully. As his grades were satisfactory, even if it was immediately obvious this wouldn't be his number one asset, he was unsurprisingly one of the 22 players selected from among the 2,000 candidates. He would come to us on Sunday nights to train every day at Clairefontaine, while attending school with a tailored curriculum at the Collège Catherine de Vivonne in Rambouillet. On Friday nights, he would return to his family in Bondy and play during the weekend at his club, where he was above his age category with the U15s in his first year, then the U17s the following season.'

Despite his young age – he was not yet thirteen when he joined the INF – Kylian quickly took the measure of his new life. At the Clairefontaine boarding school, he began by sharing a room with Armand Lauriente, another striker from Sarcelles, then moved in the second year to share with Khamis Digol N'Dozangue, a defender who went to AJ Auxerre. Very quickly, between card games of Crazy Eights and shooting the breeze about football, his personality made him very popular: 'Yep, he was always the first to make jokes and would keep going on about them,' confirms Kilian Bevis, who has since returned to the world of amateur football. 'We gave him plenty of nicknames: there was "*El Bébé*", because he liked to pout, and "Peanuts" because of the shape of his head.'

'Kylian was a joker and one of the first to set the mood by making fun of others, particularly during our impromptu song "battles" on the bus from school to training!' explains Yann Kitala, a striker who turned professional in 2017 at Olympique Lyonnais. 'We were like brothers. We thought about football all day every day. We would play one-on-one in our rooms and when that wasn't enough we'd sneak over the balcony at night to play five-a-side in the grounds. As there weren't any lights, we had to use our phones!'

At the Clairefontaine complex, where the twenty or

so trainees from the 1998 group trained every afternoon after classes under the watchful eye of Jean-Claude Lafargue, Kylian discovered competition: 'At Bondy, he was the star of his team, the best at his club and in his league, but at the INF, he found himself among players at the same level as him or even better,' says one of his former teammates. 'It's true that it wasn't always easy for him during the two years he spent with us,' continues Gérard Prêcheur. 'At amateur clubs, strikers aren't asked to defend very much. Here, he found himself surrounded by the best players in the Paris region. It pushed him to surpass himself in order to improve his game, both as an individual and as part of a team.'

During his time at Clairefontaine, Kylian would have to show real strength of character because, as the months went on, the agreement made in the summer of 2011 with Stade Malherbe Caen became more and more shaky. The Normandy club were in great difficulty on the footballing front and their budget had been cut. 'By the end of his first year at the INF, no documents had yet been signed. We wanted to do something but it dragged on and the situation eventually became more difficult when our club was relegated to Ligue 2 at the end of the 2011–12 season,' says Laurent Glaize, with a note of bitterness. 'Talks with the family were still continuing, but after a while the directors at Caen asked me to let go. The president at the time, Jean-François Fortin, always protected his employees.

He had the choice between spending €60,000 a year for a thirteen-year-old player or keeping on one or two of the club's staff members. The calculations were made quickly, even if Kylian's arrival would have been a real investment for the club. They asked me to let the family know and, during the 2012–13 season, I told them about the decision over the phone. On the other end of the line, Fayza replied: "What are we supposed to do now? I told all the other clubs that we were signing with you!" I have to say that it was the toughest moment in my career, saying no to Kylian Mbappé!'

What did Caen's about-turn matter? The little prodigy from Seine-Saint-Denis would soon find himself at the top of many club's wish lists as they had sensed the change in the prevailing wind direction. Kylian would have the opportunity to keep a promise made on his tenth birthday to his uncle Pierre Mbappé, when he gave him a model of the Santiago-Bernabeu stadium. 'One day it'll be me who takes you to a box at Real Madrid,' the boy said confidently to those who had come to watch him blow out his candles. At the time, everyone laughed and gently made fun of him. But four years later, his crazy dream would become a reality. Kylian was apparently spotted by a Real Madrid scout in November 2012 during a match in the white shirt of the INF Clairefontaine. At least, that was what the head of recruitment at the Spanish club told Wilfrid when he called to invite his son for a week's trial in Madrid. 'It fell right in the week of his birthday,' his parents told the local press. 'So, we didn't go to Spain to find out more about his potential but to give him a treat.'

Real Madrid took care of hosting the family – who were accompanied for the occasion by loyal uncle, Pierre Mbappé and long-standing friend, Alain Mboma – as only the big clubs know how. When they came out of the airport on 16 December 2012, a driver was waiting to take the small group to the hotel. Kylian gave a blow-by-blow account of the rest of the trip to a French weekly: 'The first day, we had seats to watch a Liga game against Espanyol. The next morning we went to the academy. Monsieur Zidane showed us around a bit, then I took part in my first training session. We just had to play! I also played in a match. On the fourth day, I was doing a warm-down session and I saw the players. I had my photo taken with all of them!'

In one of the pictures taken at the Valdebebas training centre, Kylian is wearing a Real Madrid tracksuit, arm in arm with his childhood idol, Cristiano Ronaldo. Despite the 2–2 draw conceded a few days earlier, the Portuguese player was in good humour with a broad smile. At his side, Kylian does not seem at all intimidated and is holding up two fingers in a victory sign. This meeting with the multiple Ballon d'Or-winner would long represent the finest trophy of his visit to Madrid.

Back in the Paris region, Kylian told his friends every

last detail of the incredible adventure he had just been on: 'He told us about meeting Zidane, and Ronaldo, of course. He showed us the photos, but without boasting,' remembers Théo Suner. 'Of course, it made us dream, but we soon realised that stories like that are rare and don't happen to everyone.'

But the red carpet laid out by Real Madrid and the presence of a former French star among their ranks was not enough to turn the heads of the Mbappé clan. As in 2011, after the trip to Chelsea, reason prevailed in the end: 'We haven't changed our minds. Even if Zinedine Zidane did look after us and told us about their plans for Kylian, we're going to stay in our place and keep our heads on our shoulders,' reported Pierre Mbappé in an interview, not necessarily impressed to see his nephew courted by one of the biggest clubs in the world. 'Even today, people are still asking me why Kylian didn't go to Real. It's simple. Because he was very young at the time and there was no guarantee it would work. People don't realise the huge upheaval it would have meant for a fourteen-year-old boy. He would have had to have adapted to a new language, a new club and it would have involved a categorical change of life for the entire family. There was plenty of discussion and a choice was made.'

And that choice would not be in favour of the *Casa Blanca*. Nor of Manchester City, the second English club to enter the race after Chelsea. In France, the

Girondins de Bordeaux would also be sent packing, as were Paris Saint-Germain, who, like Pierre Reynaud, their iconic scout in Île de France, had never really given up since first making contact in 2009. All these contenders would be pipped at the post by a second division club, AS Monaco.

In the spring of 2013, the club from the principality was in the process of returning to France's top flight and, above all, had colossal financial means at its disposal, having been bought eighteen months earlier by the Russian billionaire Dmitry Rybolovlev. A new plan was underway to build a team that could compete on the European stage, with a combination of well-known players and young hopefuls. In order to attract Kylian Mbappé, AS Monaco also had another asset up their sleeve: the presence at the club of a certain … Reda Hammache! The man who had spotted Kylian for Rennes and put the pressure on to attract him to Lens had joined the ASM recruitment team led by Souleymane Camara that season: 'As soon as I found out Kylian was back on the market, I got in touch with the family and told them: "You're free, I'm at a new club, so what are we waiting for?" To begin with, Wilfrid and Fayza weren't all that open to the idea. The distance frightened them a bit and they hadn't had a particularly good experience when they were in contact with the club a few years earlier. I told them that the whole management team had changed and ended up convincing them to meet my boss Souleymane Camara and the director of the academy, Frédéric Barilaro. It clicked immediately, as they knew how to talk to parents and present a plan that was consistent with Kylian's ambitions.'

On 3 July 2013, after four years of negotiations, plenty of twists and turns and two great years spent at the National Football Institute in Clairefontaine, Kylian Mbappé officially signed for a professional club. The agreement sealed at the family home in Bondy, in the presence of Reda Hammache and Souleymane Camara, provided for a three-year apprentice contract and a signing bonus above €400,000, according to some sources. 'In 90 per cent of cases and given the complexity of the case, we would have felt relief and obvious joy. But we didn't, not at all. No one was jumping up and down. We took pictures of Kylian with his AS Monaco number 7 shirt. Then we moved on to something else. As far as the family and the boy were concerned, it was just the next step.'

Chapter 6

The hell of paradise

The principality of Monaco sits on a piece of land sandwiched between France and Italy. From the *moyenne corniche* coast road taken by tourists from Nice once spring arrives, the horizon is endless. The blue of the Mediterranean stretches as far as the eye can see, wrinkled by a few white streaks left by the many boats cruising off the coast. From up here, the spectacle is striking, even if it is ruined by the concrete tower blocks that suggest that even the least important square metre here has an inestimable value. And this is not just an impression. After the Vatican, Monaco is the smallest independent state in the world. Across just two square kilometres, it has a unique density of 40,000 inhabitants, three-quarters of them foreigners, and a wealth that spreads to every street corner.

From its royal palace up on Le Rocher, above the port of Fontvieille, the Grimaldi family seems to have been enjoying the spectacle for generations. The principality is a life-sized amusement park, where you can window shop for the most prestigious brands, encounter colourful British and Italian supercars at any moment, and laugh at the onlookers fixed to the spot outside the luxury hotels and casinos from which extravagantly dressed couples emerge at all times of the day and night.

Monaco is a bit over the top; not much like real life, but a waking dream enhanced by the exploits of some great champions: Ayrton Senna, six-time winner of the Formula One Grand Prix that makes the walls of the city reverberate every year; Rafael Nadal, who is at home here after winning on the clay courts of Monte-Carlo on eleven occasions; and Lionel Messi and Cristiano Ronaldo, who, since 2010, have shared UEFA's player of the year trophy awarded at the end of August during the Champions League draw at the Grimaldi Forum. At the entrance to the city, the Stade Louis II is no exception: this majestic, modern stadium in the Fontvieille area has witnessed the exploits of some of the greatest athletes, from Sergey Bubka to Usain Bolt. Since the 1980s, this 18,000-seater stadium has also played host to the matches of AS Monaco. It has seen great strikers such as Brazil's Sonny Anderson, Liberian George Weah, the Spaniard Fernando Morientes and France's 1998 world champions Yuri Djorkaeff, Thierry Henry and David Trezeguet don the famous diagonal red and white shirt.

During the summer of 2013, for its return to Ligue 1, the club carried on this tradition by recruiting a number of world-class forwards: Colombians Radamel Falcao

and James Rodriguez were wrestled away from Atlético
Madrid and FC Porto for a total sum of €105 million.
The French player Anthony Martial, not yet eighteen,
was also pilfered from Olympique Lyonnais for €5 million. In this context, the signing of Kylian Mbappé, a
young hopeful aged almost fifteen, might have gone
unnoticed on the Rock. Not at all; as is rarely the case
for such a young player, his arrival was marked by a
small sidebar in the *France Football* magazine, providing an opportunity for ASM's new recruit to talk about
his ambitions with a twist on a quote by Oscar Wilde:
'Shoot for the moon; if you miss, you'll fall on a cloud.'

During his first season at the club, the phenomenon from AS Bondy would soon find himself back
on *terra firma*. The high life would have to wait. Kylian
was housed alongside his teammates. He moved into
his accommodation underneath the arches of the
Stade Louis II, where about twenty rooms are made
available to young recruits, mostly from Marseille or
Paris. Every morning, they would climb into a mini-
bus headed for La Turbie, a small French town about
ten kilometres from the principality to spend the day
at the academy. The morning was dedicated to school
work, where Year 11 classes were given on site. In the
middle of the afternoon, it was time for training, carried out on a magnificent artificial pitch in the village
of La Turbie, looking out over the Mediterranean. It
was here, under the orders of Bruno Irlès, a former

AS Monaco defender between 1994 and 2001, and in the company of about twenty players from the 1997 and 1998 generations that Kylian would discover the national U17 league.

'From those very first sessions, and during the early season training camp at Autrans in the Vercors Massif in particular, I could see what great qualities he had,' explains Bruno Irlès, who took over the age category in 2013 after spending two years as Frédéric Barilaro's interim as head of the academy. 'He immediately showed great potential going forward, in his footwork and technical ease with the ball. I also quickly noticed deficiencies in his defensive work, an area where he didn't make any effort at all. But he wasn't even fifteen and I was counting on the season to help him progress. I thought I had time, it was his first year in the French U17 league and I wanted to incorporate him gradually, along with the other players born in 1998.'

For his first games in the national U17 league, Kylian was rarely in the starting eleven. He played intermittently and had to content himself with the end of a few matches. He was experiencing competition at his club for the first time, from older players who already had a year's experience at that level. He also had to deal with the choices and comments made by his coach, who continued to point out his lack of defensive investment. On 8 September 2013, Bruno Irlès decided to send his young recruit to the amateur section to strengthen the team playing in the U17 Division d'Honneur. It would turn out to be the first source of conflict.

'I thought it would be a good idea because it would give him the opportunity to get some playing time and experience football that was less technical but more physical. I got it wrong and it went very badly,' remembers Bruno Irlès, who detailed the incident: 'It was noted in the match report that he had made a hand gesture towards his coach, who had asked him to track back and defend. The reaction was basically saying "Leave me alone!" More surprisingly, it wasn't him who was summoned the following week, it was me! Frédéric Barilaro and Souleymane Camara had received a phone call from Kylian's parents, who couldn't understand why I'd sent their son to play in the Division d'Honneur. The result was that they told me not to make him play at that level again, when practically all the players went to the U17DH to toughen up.'

'It's true that we told him not to, but you have to remember that Kylian had already played in the U17DH in the previous season with Bondy. So there was no point in him going back down to that category,' confirms the former head of recruitment at Monaco, Souleymane Camara, who has since moved away from the world of football to join the French clay pigeon shooting federation.

Even if the player's entourage had won its case, the turn that his first few months at AS Monaco had taken was very concerning: 'In Bondy, we were wondering what was happening and had a feeling it might be about to go pear-shaped,' remembers Fanfan Suner. 'Irlès asked Kylian to defend, but is that what they ask Messi to do at Barcelona? Of course, you have to get back to your position, but you can't use players where it feels unnatural to them or ask a striker to defend like crazy.'

Wilfrid Mbappé was following developments closely. He had taken a year's sabbatical and left Fayza and Ethan in the house in Seine-Saint-Denis to move into an apartment close to the training centre in the nearby town of Cap d'Ail. He barely missed any of his son's sessions and this experienced instructor was frankly not happy with what he saw: 'He didn't like the methods used by Bruno Irlès,' according to someone close to the family. 'He said he would use a stream of abusive words on the pitch. The weaker ones would apparently cry themselves to sleep at night. Kylian was coping, although he cracked sometimes. Luckily, he had the support of his stable family and friends, who did not let it go and were constantly asking for explanations.'

A second meeting, this time in the presence of the parents, was organised in December at the La Turbie training centre. The bad feeling had not diminished, quite the contrary, and Bruno Irlès was summoned to explain himself: 'First of all, I was criticised for Kylian's lack of playing time. I replied that I'd been banned from making him play with the amateurs and that he didn't have the right mindset yet to be in the starting eleven for the U17 National League. They also told me it was my fault that the boy was unhappy but that wasn't true. Kylian was getting on well with the group, but of course he was disappointed when I didn't pick him. Lastly, they talked to me about harassment during the training sessions. I replied that an instructor has to be able to shake up a player sometimes when he's not listening to instructions or not making an effort for his teammates. That was the case with Kylian and, as I wasn't allowed to send him to the amateurs, I had to find other ways to get through to him. So yes, sometimes I would tell him "Stop playing like a star!", or "You're not at Real Madrid here, move your ass!" If I was persistent, it was to maintain my point of view and get Kylian on an equal footing with the rest of the players.'

This meeting failed to fix anything and the power struggle between the player's family and the coach of the U17 squad would continue throughout the second half of the season. 'The situation was a good example of the complexity of the profession of instructor,' analyses Marc Westerloppe, who went from the RC Lens academy to that of Paris Saint-Germain in the summer of 2013. 'Being an instructor is a bit like being a father. He has to be able to yell at his player but also know how to encourage and understand him. Of course, he had to shake Kylian sometimes and tell him: "Hey, being a footballer is a real job. You can't just go to sleep like that!" But you also had to remember that his talent had been recognised all over France, and that he was very young in the year. At that time, he still needed an emotional bond, to feel warmth, and that may have been what was missing.'

'It was clear that Irlès, who was also in conflict with Barilaro at the same time, failed to win the player over,' confirms Reda Hammache. 'But there was no question of accusing him either. All instructors have problems with players sometimes. It was unlucky for Irlès that it happened with Mbappé, the player with the biggest media spotlight on him at the time.'

Relations deteriorated definitively in the spring of 2014 during the Montaigu tournament played in the west of France, near Nantes. On 21 April, in the last match of the competition against the Girondins de Bordeaux, Irlès claimed Kylian had reacted inappropriately: 'When I said something about replacing him, he made a gesture with his arm as if to say "Get lost!" I took him off the pitch immediately, without any explanation. It was his last official match. He never played with me again.' According to some sources, Irlès and the player's uncle, Pierre Mbappé, (almost) came to blows. 'I don't want to go into details, but it went too far that time. So I went to speak to the management to explain my decision to exclude him from my squad.'

It is not hard to imagine the club's predicament, caught between a rock and a hard place: they could not go against their instructor, but at the same time needed to retain the confidence of the Mbappé family, whom, some believed, had decided to look elsewhere if a solution was not found quickly. To bring an end to the conflict, the director of the academy Frédéric Barilaro was supported by the club's new sporting director, the Portuguese Luis Campos. The two men apparently found the right words to reassure the family after what had been an extraordinary season. After training by himself for a week in the company of the assistant coach Sylvain Legwinski, Kylian would finish the season with Barilaro's U19 squad.

A few weeks later, as expected, Bruno Irlès left AS Monaco to prepare for his qualification as a professional coach, which would take him to Arles-Avignon and then to FC Sheriff Tiraspol in Moldova. He left his long-standing club with some regrets about 'not having been able to help Kylian make progress with his weaknesses, even if the year would still have helped him toughen up mentally'. Kylian would finish his first season in the France U17 league with 1,175 minutes spent on the pitch, half the possible playing time. Irlès would also come across some statistics in the notes he wrote at the time: five goals scored, including two against Nîmes, three assists and … two direct errors that resulted in a goal. 'Yep, I make a note of what's bad as well as what's good. You don't get the chance to go back and do it over!'

Chapter 7

Better than Thierry Henry

He was the ultimate benchmark at Monaco. Whenever a mixed-race striker, or one with West Indian roots, began raking up goals for the youth team, he was heralded as the new Thierry Henry. But the comparison did not often last long as it was hard to compete with the former French international who had spent time in the principality between 1993 and 1999. He had scored 42 goals in the French U17 league during his first season at the club and went on to set several records for his age: for his professional debut at the age of seventeen years and fourteen days, followed by his first Ligue 1 goal, scored on 29 April 1995 against Lens at seventeen years, eight months and twelve days.

Kylian had been hearing about Thierry Henry from an early age: on the pitches at Bondy, spectators along the touchlines would often see him as the new 'Titi' whenever he set off on long runs with the ball at his feet; when he arrived at the INF Clairefontaine in 2011, the director, Gérard Prêcheur also quickly made the connection: 'It's a rare thing at thirteen; they both already combined speed and technique. With Thierry Henry it was his physical qualities that prevailed, whereas for Kylian it was his talent as a dribbler that emerged first.' And, naturally, the parallel continued during his first few years at Monaco: 'They do have plenty in common in terms of their origins and history, but for me, that's where it stops,' says Bruno Irlès, who, before coaching Mbappé, had played alongside Thierry Henry at Monaco and for the France Under 21 team. 'It's not a criticism, but Thierry Henry was a hard-worker. Even though he had a huge career with Juventus, Barcelona, the New York Red Bulls and Arsenal, of course, he always had to work hard and constantly keep challenging himself. Kylian doesn't at all. With him, it's pure talent.'

But it still took a season for the prodigy from Île-de-France to take stock of his ambitions and the expectations of his Monegasque instructors. After a difficult start with Bruno Irlès, his second year would be much more enjoyable: 'He had got used to how the training centre worked and was fully integrated into the squad,' explains the former head of recruitment, Souleymane Camara. 'With a team of instructors who were much more in line with his way of thinking, he felt freer and soon regained his confidence. And when Kylian is happy, that's often when he does exceptional things.'

Proof of this came in the form of the first match in the France U17 league season, when the former

Bondy player scored twice in ASM's 6–2 win away at their neighbours OGC Nice. During the first half of the 2014–15 season, when he was still not yet sixteen, Kylian played above his category for Frédéric Barilaro's U19 team on several occasions. 'He felt as if he could make the difference and perhaps he felt more valued,' remembers one of his former teammates at the training centre. 'Perhaps the work done in the previous season was also starting to pay off.'

By late December, Kylian had already scored eight goals in the France U17 league and twice with the U19s, away at Furiani in Corsica and at Lyon in a game that ended in a 2–2 draw. He had also made a remarkable start in the UEFA Youth League – the U19s Champions League – providing an assist late in Monaco's 3–1 loss to the Russian team Zenit Saint Petersburg. During the second half of the season, he would barely leave Frédéric Barilaro's squad, scoring six more goals, including two against AC Ajaccio. 'We'd had a great season and we finished with the best attack in our group,' remembers the centre forward Irvin Cardona. 'There was some competition but, even though he was the youngest, Kylian kept us entertained.'

But his teammates had not seen anything yet: the 2015–16 season would be a record breaker … On a summer visit to the shores of the Mediterranean, a family friend would struggle to recognise the young entertainer from Bondy: 'He'd become calm, mature and serious. His voice had begun to break. He was no longer a kid, he'd taken a step forward.' On 3 October, after only seven U19 league games, Kylian had already scored ten goals and provided two assists, combined with the *tour de force* of scoring two goals in each of the first four games, against Toulouse, Arles-Avignon, Bastia and Gazélec Ajaccio. 'I got wind of his performances and went straight to watch the Monaco game at Clermont-Ferrand in the Auvergne. I saw a boy who was completely transformed,' says Marc Westerloppe, who had by then been working within PSG's recruitment structure for more than two years. 'He was ready for the top level. He'd grown and his muscles were beginning to form. There was a feeling that something would happen once he'd gained a few kilos.'

In mid-October, the sixteen-year-old kid made his debut with the reserve team in the CFA league, France's fourth division. Just a few minutes to start with, against US Colomiers, then, a fortnight later, a first start against Hyères, before finally scoring two goals in quick succession in mid-November against Pau and Mont-de-Marsan, with the added bonus of an assist.

'It was at that time that we began to take notice of the phenomenon, seeing his name feature prominently in the match reports every weekend,' explains the journalist Fabien Pigalle from his offices at *Monaco-Matin*. 'At that time, the Monaco attack wasn't working all that well and they were looking for new faces. A few weeks after having been mentioned for the first time in an article, he appeared at training with the professionals.' In the space of three and a half months, the kid from Allée des Lilas had gone from the U19 squad to that of Ligue 1. In mid-November, during an international break, Mbappé took advantage of the absence of numerous more experienced players, who were either injured or responding to call ups from their national teams, to join the squad managed by Leonardo Jardim. And that was where he stayed.

'At the start of the session, the players asked me if I was on trial,' the teenager would remember a few months later. 'When I told them I was sixteen, they were a bit shocked. They thought I was three years older. The coach also asked me if I was new. I told him that I'd been here for three years. After training, he told me to come back the next day and asked for my father's phone number.'

Jardim had fallen under the spell of the new phenomenon from the academy. He was determined to throw him in at the deep end as soon as possible. On 29 November 2015, Kylian was called up to the professional squad for the first time for the trip to Marseille. Three days later, on 2 December, his big moment finally arrived: Kylian made his first steps in Ligue 1 against Stade Malherbe Caen, replacing Portuguese defender Fábio Coentrão in the dying moments of the game. With the number 33 on his back, he stepped out onto the pitch of the Louis II in the 88th minute.

Kylian would not change the course of the match, which ended in a disappointing 1–1 draw, but he did change the course of history: at the age of sixteen years, eleven months and twelve days, he became the youngest player for his club to play for the first team, and wiped Thierry Henry from the record books for the first time. 'Of course, it made an impression on people,' confirms the journalist from the *Fast Foot* blog, Damien Chedeville. 'He had just surpassed Thierry Henry, who had been the ultimate benchmark at the club for many years. And eight days later, Kylian also provided his first assist on his debut in the Europa League against Tottenham.'

The records just kept tumbling: on 20 February 2016, during his ninth appearance for the first team, Kylian found his way to goal for the first time, scoring against Troyes to make it 3–1 in injury time. About ten minutes after coming on, he took advantage of a good pick-up by Helder Costa and a return pass from the Portuguese midfielder to surge into the area, before striking a low shot with his left foot and wrong-footing the keeper. It would take a few seconds for him to realise what had happened. The time to glance over to the official stand, where even the Mbappé family could not believe their eyes. At seventeen years and two months, Kylian had just pulled off a major feat. He had become the youngest professional goal scorer in the history of AS Monaco. Thierry Henry had once again been relegated to second position.

'Kylian has always needed challenges. Since a very young age, he's always had targets in his head and done everything he could to reach them as soon as possible,' confirms a relative. 'This first professional goal was further proof. It was also a surprise because, at that time, the family were in the midst of negotiations with the Monaco directors.'

The three-year training-apprentice contract signed with Monaco in 2013 would expire at the end of June and, just four months before this deadline, AS Monaco had still not 'locked in' its player by formalising his first professional contract. Time was running out for the principality club, which was once again facing competition from some of the biggest clubs in Europe: 'Since October and his performances for the U19s, several clubs had begun to position themselves, thinking they had a good chance to pick up the player without the need to pay a transfer fee,' says a recruiter from a French club. 'Kylian's rise in power had done nothing to help that. Monaco were trapped and under attack from all sides.'

Real Madrid, Bayern Munich, Borussia Dortmund, Olympique Lyonnais and Paris Saint-Germain were the clubs that had been named in the press since the end of 2015. 'After seeing him at Clermont-Ferrand, I alerted my managers at PSG that the opportunity might be about to present itself,' confirms Marc Westerloppe. Several meetings took place in Paris between the player's family and the director of football at the time, Olivier Létang, who was already envisaging a five-year plan. At the same time, several English clubs entered the arena: Chelsea and Manchester United argued their case, as did Liverpool, but it was Arsenal, Thierry Henry's former club, who showed the greatest interest. Scouts from the Gunners were spotted in the principality on several occasions and their iconic French manager, Arsène Wenger, even travelled to the Paris region to try to convince Kylian's family.

Faced with all these contenders, AS Monaco did not sit idly by. Behind the scenes, the club was busy looking for an alternative solution that could soften the blow, with an attempt to recruit the Rennes player Ousmane Dembélé, who was reluctant to sign his first professional contract with the club where he had trained. But ASM did not give up, taking more and more meetings with Wilfrid and Fayza. The technical director Claude Makélélé and President Vadim Vasilyev repeatedly revised their financial proposals upwards and, according to *Nice-Matin*, the signing bonus had risen from €1 million to €1.6 million in the space of just a few weeks. But what was of primary interest to the Mbappé clan were footballing guarantees and the amount of playing time Kylian would get with the first team. 'It was for that reason that, despite higher financial offers, PSG and Arsenal didn't manage to sign the player because those clubs couldn't guarantee Kylian a place in the starting eleven,' suggests a journalist who followed the affair closely.

Perhaps it was his first professional goal scored against Troyes in mid-February that changed the outcome of the saga. After taking the time to integrate the promising striker into his training sessions, that night Leonardo Jardim became convinced once and for all of the player's potential and decided to give him a preferred position in his squad. By way of proof, on 28 February at the Stade de la Beaujoire in Nantes, Jardim selected Kylian for his first start in Ligue 1, putting him on the right of the attacking quartet of João Moutinho, Diego Carillo and Thomas Lemar. In passing, the Portuguese manager also made a point of telling the newcomer: 'Give me two years of your career and you'll see the player you'll become.'

The staff at AS Monaco began paying more attention, followed several days later by the decisive intervention from the club's sporting director, Luis Campos: 'I saw Kylian's mother at training a few moments after Vadim Vasilyev agreed to let me take over the case. It was like a sign from God. I spent 40 minutes with her and explained the advantages and disadvantages of going to a big club at such an early stage. At PSG or Arsenal, he would arrive in a dressing room made up of big personalities and egos and no one would speak to him. The players would say: "Who is this kid?" No, he needed to wait a bit, until the day when he would open the dressing room doors at a big club and the other players would say: "Welcome, Kylian. We really like you and we're going to help you."'

On 6 March 2016, AS Monaco formalised the signing of Kylian Mbappé's first professional contract. In the statement published on the club's official website, Vice President Vadim Vasilyev welcomed the positive outcome: 'With Kylian attracting interest from some very big clubs, this agreement is further proof of the appeal of our project, where young talents can find their place. It is also a tribute to the work of the AS Monaco Academy. I have every confidence that with plenty of hard work, he can become a player of great talent.'

AS Monaco had been able to put into place the conditions to keep their player and make the financial effort required: the three-year professional contract was accompanied by a signing bonus of €3 million for the player and a starting salary of €85,000, which would be re-evaluated to €100,000 and then €120,000 over the next two seasons. It was a vote of confidence that Kylian would succeed in repaying magnificently during the last few months of the season.

Chapter 8

Passed with merit

The AS Monaco TV cameraman was on standby to get Kylian's first impressions. He was not, however, at the exit to the dressing rooms at the Stade Louis II but in the corridors of a national education examination centre, where the French striker had just finished the first part of his 2016 *baccalauréat* exam. Carrying a black backpack and wearing a plain jumper, the new pearl of Monaco looked like an ordinary teenager, but, for a seventeen-year-old high-school student, he was already very comfortable in front of the camera when asked to comment on the subject he had just been working on for more than three hours. Philosophy is not the subject with the greatest weighting in the Science and Technology of Management (STMG) stream but Kylian did not skip it: 'I chose the second question: "Can we justify our beliefs?" It's related to football and that's what I know best,' he fired back at the journalist with a broad smile.

'Can we realise our dreams?' would undoubtedly have been a more appropriate title given the events shaking up the life of the kid from Bondy at the end of the 2015–16 season.

Three weeks earlier, Kylian had achieved the Holy Grail for any player from an academy. Alongside his friends from the generations born in 1997 and 1998, he had won the Coupe Gambardella in a final – played on Saturday 21 May at the Stade de France in the Parisian suburb of Saint-Denis – during which he had reached another level.

With the crazy year he had been having coupled with his incredible rise, Kylian had logically been spared the first few rounds of the French Under 19 cup. While his friends had fought to get past Rodez, Clermont-Ferrand, Metz and Caen, he was continuing his apprenticeship at the highest level, celebrating his second Ligue 1 start in March with a fine 2–0 win over PSG at the Parc des Princes, then marking his four-teenth appearance in the professional team on 10 April in Lille with his second assist.

'When he joined us for the semi-final, we knew it would give us more weight,' said his great friend from the training centre, Irvin Cardona, a player with a styl-ish blonde haircut. 'Despite the steps forward he had been making, we were still very close. We were always on the phone. We also knew his mindset, even if he did now have a new status after ten games played with the professional team. We knew he would still give every-thing for his friends.'

(*above*) Kylian Mbappé of Monaco celebrates after opening the scoring against Manchester City in the UEFA Champions League round of sixteen second leg match played at Stade Louis II, Monaco on 15 March 2017. (Kieran McManus/BPI/Shutterstock)

(*right*) Shaking hands with Manchester City manager Pep Guardiola at full time in the UEFA Champions League round of sixteen second leg match between AS Monaco and Manchester City played at Stade Louis II, Monaco. (Kieran McManus/BPI/Shutterstock)

Prince Albert II of Monaco congratulates MBappé as Monaco are crowned Ligue 1 champions for the first time since 2000. (AP/Shutterstock)

(L–R) Andrea Raggi, Kylian Mbappé, Valère Germain, Leonardo Jardim, Radamel Falcao and Danijel Subašić celebrate winning Ligue 1 at the Prince's Palace of Monaco, May 2017. (OLIVIER ANRIGO/ EPA/Shutterstock)

Scoring his first senior goal for the France national team in August 2017, netting the fourth in a 4–0 victory over the Netherlands in a FIFA World Cup qualifier.
(James Marsh/BPI/Shutterstock)

Being unveiled at Parc des Princes after sealing his record-breaking move from Monaco to PSG. Pictured holding the shirt alongside his brother Ethan and his father.
(Alfonso Jimenez/Shutterstock)

(*above*) Celebrating scoring his side's fourth goal with his familiar arms-crossed celebration in France's 4–2 World Cup final victory against Croatia at the Luzhniki Stadium, Moscow. (Martin Meissner/AP/Shutterstock)

Mbappé kisses the trophy as France lift the World Cup for only the second time in their history, on 15 July 2018. (Matthias Schrader/AP/Shutterstock)

On 23 April in Libourne, in the south-west of France, where the competition's semi-finals were held, AS Monaco overcame Stade Brestois as expected. But the victory was a long time coming and Kylian initially had some trouble with his movement and positioning when calling for the ball. Not surprising, given that he had not had the opportunity for a squad training session with his teammates since returning to youth football. 'The day before, he was still training with the pros before finding out he would leave that afternoon to join up with the Gambardella squad,' remembers Fabien Pigalle, who was closely following the progress of the U19s for the *Monaco-Matin* daily. Kylian's presence in Libourne was obviously not good news for the team from Brest: 'My players were really frightened of him, although we hadn't focused on him during our match preparations,' admitted the opposition coach, Éric Assadourian. 'During the game, he was better than everyone else and caused us a lot of problems. We were dealing with a future great.'

Just before half-time, Kylian took advantage of one of his first chances to open the scoring with a diagonal strike.

His partner upfront, Irvin Cardona, took charge of the second goal of the game after an hour of play to guarantee AS Monaco's place in the final of the competition.

'We'd made it to the Stade de France! I'm from

Paris, so playing there means a lot to me. I've seen France play there and been to watch other Gambardella finals,' said the delighted star of the 1998 generation after the final whistle. 'Now we've got one game left, and, as they say, you don't play a final, you win it!'

A month later, Kylian proved these statements were not just hot air. He would be the number one architect of his club's fourth success in the Coupe Gambardella. Against Racing Club de Lens, he was unstoppable during the 90 minutes played as a curtain raiser to the final of the Coupe de France between Paris Saint-Germain and Olympique de Marseille. 'We had the opportunity to see plenty of talent on display in the Gambardella final … But Benzema and Ben Arfa had never been on another level in that way,' said a member of the French Football Federation. 'A lot is expected of great players at that age in a final and they often feel inhibited by what's at stake. Not Mbappé. He was already on another planet!'

Before the game, with plenty of calm and tact, he agreed to appear on live French television with the veteran journalist Daniel Auclair, in charge of interviewing the teams just before they stepped out onto the pitch at the Stade de France: 'It was a rare moment on television,' said Damien Chedeville, author of the *Fast Foot* blog, with a note of humour. 'The France Télévision journalist, who was an old hand, really screwed things up by mistaking Kylian for the captain of Racing Club de Lens, Taylor Moore. It was something that would have thrown plenty of young players, but not him. Mbappé put him right without raising an eyebrow at the journalist's mistake and gave a clear and precise answer. The funny situation showed his mental strength and how smart he was. He was already tough for his age.'

Kylian also showed on the pitch that he was no longer just a youth team player. Wearing the red and white shirt of AS Monaco, he seemed to be enjoying himself in a Stade de France that still sounded empty. The team from Lens did not know how to stop him. In the 29th minute, Kylian took advantage of a slip by his marker on the left wing to rush into the opposing team's midfield, stare down their central defence and delicately provide a pass, between two players, to his friend Irvin Cardona, who finished the move with a magnificent left-footed jab. This first goal was not only the result of talent but also of an incredible understanding between the two strikers. 'It's true that things were always easy with Kylian,' recognised the first goal scorer in the final, on loan during the 2017–18 season to Cercle Brugge in the Belgian first division. 'I don't know if I'll ever get to play with him again, but he's probably the person I've had the best understanding with on a football pitch.'

Irvin Cardona would have a front row seat in the second half to see the number 10 score two goals on the pitch at the Stade de France for the first time: in the

47th minute, Kylian took advantage of a back-heel from Cardona and a return pass from Guévin Tormin to give his right foot a second chance to do the talking, with calm precision. At the end of the final, in the 92nd minute, this time he needed no one to get past four Lens players, who were by now resigned to their fate, before scoring with a powerful shot that went in off the post and became the third and last goal of the game.

After lifting the cup and collecting his medal, Kylian spoke of his happiness: 'You can't compare how happy I'm feeling now with when I scored my first goal in L1. They're both wonderful things. But that time, I wasn't helping my teammates to win a cup. This time I was helping my friends.'

The victory would be celebrated in Paris that night: 'Kylian already had a status among that generation,' said a team insider. 'He wasn't treated like a prince but he did get some privileges. He went home after the game with his parents and joined the group a bit later, during a meal in a restaurant that was also a nightclub. Most of them hadn't been out that much before and were very shy, but Kylian had a real self-confidence, particularly when it came to going up to girls. Just like when he's on the pitch, you could feel that he had a real natural ease and confidence.'

For almost all of this golden generation from AS Monaco, the evening represented the climax of the season and ushered in a well-deserved holiday.

For everyone that is except Kylian, who never does what everyone else does.

The incredible second half of the 2015–16 season had also been marked by a misunderstanding with the French Football Federation that had dragged on for almost three years: Kylian had not played any official matches for the France U16 team in 2013, had made only two appearances in an U17 blue shirt in September 2014 against Ukraine and then almost nothing until he was called up in January 2016 for the Copa del Atlántico in Spain, which he would eventually be unable to honour due to an unusual injury (testicular torsion). How had the France manager, Jean-Claude Giuntini, been able to do without the services of the greatest young player of his generation, quickly pigeon-holing him as a 'bit part' player? Although the national coach refused to expand on the subject, others had ideas: 'Like others before him, Giuntini was annoyed by Kylian's character; Jean-Claude Lafargue at the INF Clairefontaine then Bruno Irlès at Monaco had also interpreted his confidence and natural manner as self-importance. But to get to the top level, you have to have that self-confidence. Just look at Zlatan Ibrahimović and Cristiano Ronaldo!'

'During my year with Kylian in 2013, I had had Giuntini on the phone to debrief from a pre-selection camp for the France team. Apparently, it hadn't gone well enough for him to return,' confirms Bruno Irlès. 'You also have to remember the background and the trauma of the 2010 World Cup in South Africa. After the scandal in Knysna, the instructors started question- ing themselves and decided that talent wasn't every- thing, you also had to take into account the team aspect and the player's behaviour.'

As a result, Kylian would not be called up for the U17 Euros, won in 2015 by France after a 4–1 win over Germany in Bulgaria. Odsonne Édouard was pre- ferred to him upfront for the Bleuets and the Paris Saint-Germain striker scored eight goals during the competition, including a hat-trick in the final. 'It would have been a bonus if he'd been with us. Although we had some great players upfront, we were still surprised not to see him selected,' acknowledged the captain of the 1998 generation, Timothé Cognat. 'But we were very surprised to learn he was playing above his age category for the France U19 team.'

Persona non grata with the 1998 generation man- aged by Jean-Claude Giuntini, Kylian would eventu- ally find his international status with players born in 1997. In search of an attacking talent in the absence of Ousmane Dembélé, the France U19 manager, Ludovic Batelli, chose not to listen to hearsay and called him up in March 2016 for the last qualifying round of the European Championships in that age group. The idea would turn out to be a bright one. Kylian was quickly welcomed into the squad by the older players and soon became indispensable on the pitch. After a first start against Montenegro on 24 March, he made the difference in the two last qualifying games: he opened the scoring from a corner on 26 March during a big 4–0 win over Denmark; yet again, he scored the only goal three days later against Serbia in the third and decisive match that would send the Bleuets to the finals: 'Even though he was almost two years younger than some of the other players, Kylian showed an incredible maturity,' remembers Ludovic Batelli. 'He was quickly adopted not as the youngest player coming into the group, but as a great player and a great guy in the dressing room.'

These comments were confirmed by the captain of the 1997 generation, Lucas Tousart: 'Despite his young age, he immediately caught on to our way of working. His integration was very fast and we quickly realised he could really help us with the games we had coming up.'

Between 12 and 24 July 2016, Kylian brought happiness to the France team during the Euro U19s played in Germany: 'We saw him try some incredible things, like bringing down an opponent with a simple body dummy or pulling off a rainbow kick after a looping flick. He was fantastic throughout the competition,' recalls the journalist Damien Chedeville. 'He was decisive in the group games, with a stunning goal against Croatia and then two in the vital match against Holland, which we won 5–1.' Kylian was also on form during the semi-final in Mannheim on 21 July, when he took the France team through against Portugal. After Pacheco's early goal, he gave Ludovic Blas the chance to equalise on the end of a powerful surge down the left wing. In the second half, he secured the win for the Bleuets thanks to two more goals in the 67th and 75th minutes. 'It was in that game that he again showed those who doubted him that there were no limits to the progress he could make,' says the *Monaco-Matin* journalist Fabien Pigalle. On 24 July, France were crowned U19 champions of Europe, thrashing Italy 4–0. Kylian did not score, leaving this privilege to Issa Diop, Lucas Tousart, Ludovic Blas and Jean-Kévin Augustin, who would also take the tournament's golden boot.

It didn't matter, the 2015–16 season had already been more than generous. Records for his age, a first professional contract, the Coupe Gambardella and European champions, everything he touched had turned to gold! Or almost … Kylian had to wait until September to pass his STMG *baccalauréat,* for which he had fallen short by nineteen points. Proof that not even he could get everything right first time!

Chapter 9

The declaration

Kylian Mbappé, 25 April 2016: 'I'm very happy at Monaco. I'm learning a lot from my manager, Jardim. I'm surrounded by great players who support me, guide me and help me grow. For a young player like me, being at Monaco is like heaven.'

Wilfrid Mbappé, 13 October 2016: 'Without wanting to sound conceited, we don't understand the bizarre handling of Kylian in light of the promises made by the management that they would let him play as part of a rotation. Otherwise, he wouldn't have stayed. Even though he had a fantastic Euros, we weren't expecting him to become a regular in the starting eleven, we're not stupid! But we didn't think he would be the sixth-choice striker. If that's the case, we might as well go straight to a big, big club.'

What happened to make the Mbappé family overhaul their comments so radically in the space of just six months? To make Wilfrid decide to publicly question the use of his son at the start of the 2016–17 season? Perhaps it was simply a case of contrary winds beginning to blow on the shores of the Mediterranean ...

His adventure with the France U19 team had obviously encroached on his holidays, but by late July 2016 the only thing that mattered to Kylian was to resume training as quickly as possible with the professional squad, who were forced to play two qualifying matches in the middle of summer in the hope of taking part in the next Champions League. 'After the win against Italy, everyone was telling him to go out and celebrate with his teammates, but he only had one thing on his mind, going back to the hotel to recover so he could throw himself into the new season as quickly as possible,' said a France team insider.

AS Monaco even had to dampen his enthusiasm by almost forcing him to take a week off after the Euros final against Italy.

After resuming training on 30 July and missing the two games against the Turkish team Fenerbahçe that sent ASM into the Champions League play-offs, Kylian was in the starting blocks for the kick-off to the new Ligue 1 season on Friday 12 August at the Stade Louis II against En Avant de Guingamp. He was also lucky enough to be playing: in the absence of Falcao, the Brazilian Vágner Love and the French player Valère Germain, Kylian was in the starting eleven alongside Argentina's Diego Carillo. The summer evening promised to be beautiful for his first official appearance in the number 29 shirt, chosen in honour of the birthday of his little brother Ethan (29 December 2006). Unfortunately, it would turn out to be a nightmare!

In the first half, Guingamp punished the Monaco defence on two occasions. Kylian was struggling up front. He fought hard and refused to give up, as was the case in the 40th minute when he took on the defender Christophe Kerbrat. The aerial duel turned into a clash of heads. Kylian was knocked out, apparently also sustaining a jaw injury. He would not return to the pitch – replaced by Bernardo Silva – and was rushed to hospital. The diagnosis came later that evening: Kylian had suffered a concussion. He would have to observe between three weeks and a month of complete rest.

'It was obviously a blow to his season,' said a relative. 'Kylian was really hoping to keep up the positive momentum. So when he found himself at a complete standstill, given the kid's passion for the game and for competing, the weeks that followed were tough and hard to get through.'

All the more so because the absence of the new prodigy was not necessarily felt on the pitch. After eventually snatching a 2–2 draw against Guingamp, the principality team wreaked havoc in the French league in the next three games: they won 1–0 at Nantes, caused a sensation with a 4–1 win at Lille and, as a bonus, managed a prestigious home victory over Paris Saint-Germain, heavy favourites for the league title with their threatening three-pronged attack of Di María, Cavani and Lucas. Also, in the Champions League, the team that had finished third in the previous Ligue 1 season showed their strength and qualified for the group stages after a double victory over the Spanish team Villareal.

Kylian finally returned to the pitch on 10 September for a CFA league game with the reserve team: standard protocol for a young player returning after almost a month without competition. It was a return to some of his Gambardella teammates, coupled with an easy 5–1 win over ES Paulhan-Pézenas and an assist slipped in with a subtle back-heel. Kylian played for just over an hour and imagined he would rejoin the profes- sional team the following week for AS Monaco's first Champions League game against Tottenham.

'It seemed logical after a good test run with the reserve team but, three days later, he was to be disap- pointed,' said a journalist. As usual, the team sheet was revealed at the end of the last training session at La Turbie. Leonardo Jardim had called up an expanded squad of 21 players for the highly anticipated trip to White Hart Lane. But, to the amazement of those close to Kylian, his name did not appear in the line of attack, which did include Radamel Falcao, Guido Carillo and the two young French players, Valère Germain and Corentin Jean.

'He took it very badly,' confirms a family friend. 'He

was obviously hugely disappointed not to be going to London for the first Champions League game.' That was putting it mildly ... According to some sources, Kylian burst into tears when it was announced he would not be playing and even disappeared for several hours. The pill was hard to swallow, as disappointment was mixed with a failure to understand. How could the manager have overlooked him in favour of Corentin Jean, a striker on loan the previous season to Troyes and someone who had hardly been used since the start of the season? 'It is true that the choice could have seemed really surprising with hindsight,' confirmed a follower of the club. 'You have to wonder about Jardim's motivation. Was it merely a sporting choice to protect a player returning from injury or a way for the Portuguese manager to regain the upper hand after having the pace dictated the previous season by Kylian's family during negotiations for his first professional contract? Only Jardim knew the answer but what was certain was that he did have previous form: two years earlier, he had done something similar to Anthony Martial during a match at Nantes by taking him off only a few minutes after bringing him on.'

Whatever the case, the situation did not improve over the following weeks: even if Kylian was picked again in Ligue 1, he did not play at all against Rennes, Nice and Angers. The kid from Bondy sat quietly on the bench, watching for a sign from his coach that did not come. On 27 September, there was a chink of light in the grey sky of his season: he finally returned to competition in the second Champions League game. Thirteen minutes against Bayer Leverkusen that would be followed four days later by eight minutes on the pitch at FC Metz in Ligue 1. Although there had been no time for him to make his mark against the Germans, Kylian took advantage of his return to the French league to provide Gabriel Boschilia with an assist.

Twenty-one minutes of play in September added to 41 minutes in August. Even taking into account his injury, Kylian's pitch time had been paltry after two months of competition. The situation had gone on too long for the Mbappé family, who took advantage of the international break to get their message across. On 13 October 2016, Wilfrid revealed his discontent in an interview given to *L'Equipe* in which he openly denounced a period during which Kylian had been starved of playing time and clearly threatened to go elsewhere: 'This situation is not making Kylian happy and you can see it on his face during the week. I know it's bothering the club, but it doesn't stop him from working. He is ambitious, but let's judge him for what he really is: a competitor. Some will say he's only seventeen, that he needs to calm down, but it's not impatience because the club told him he was going to play. He needs to be playing at his age so we'll have to think hard about the winter transfer window.'

Once again, the Mbappé family were taking on the AS Monaco directors and were determined to assert the player's rights and to get the club to honour the commitments they had made: 'It wasn't surprising to see the father get involved,' continues our journalist. 'The family had always stood up for themselves and never allowed themselves to be swept aside when it came to saying things to protect Kylian. The declaration was not necessarily well received at the club. The directors don't like it much when a player's entourage starts making waves and the older players in the dressing room don't always look kindly on the father of a young player saying whatever he likes to their manager. But they didn't react because they were well aware of Kylian's talent in training and that he had earned his place in the starting eleven.'

Moreover, if the staff at Monaco were slow to put their trust in their budding star, other European clubs were ready to throw the doors to their dressing rooms wide open. Barcelona had enquired in August and Manchester City had made an offer of €40 million for the U19 European champion. Pep Guardiola had tried his luck but ASM did not succumb to the temptation of making a big profit. In October 2016, the German club Leipzig also tried to take advantage of the situation to pick up the player through their director of football, Ralf Rangnick: 'I'd forged a great relationship with his father. The trust was mutual and we were on the same wavelength. At the time, he told me that if I guaranteed I would be the club's next manager, he would entrust his son to me because he had confidence in me,' the German manager would explain sometime later.

But neither Leipzig, Barça nor the Citizens would succeed in pilfering the young French hopeful from the Monaco club. Twenty-four hours after the article appeared in *L'Equipe*, Kylian resumed his – sad – early-season routine. Called up by Jardim for the trip to Toulouse for the ninth game of the Ligue 1 season, he would watch his team's 3–1 defeat from the touchline. With Falcao absent, it was the duo of Carillo-Germain who were favoured once again by the Portuguese manager. This time, Kylian was not even called in as a reinforcement at the end of the game. It looked like a punishment and it certainly seemed that way when the young striker was asked to strengthen the reserve team for a trip to Pontet in the CFA league the following day. It was hardly a gift. But, better than the words spoken by his father, Kylian made his own declaration on the pitch: in 90 minutes of play, he scored two goals in the young Monaco team's 3–1 win!

Chapter 10

Louis II, 21 October 2016

The image says it all: Kylian, wearing a short-sleeved red and white shirt with both arms raised and his index fingers pointing up to the sky. His head is impeccably shaved and his black eyes are fixed on the stands. His face is calm. The former Bondy player no longer has to apologise for existing. He has probably already realised that this Friday 21 October 2016 will change the course of his young career. In the space of 90 minutes he has just demonstrated the incredible extent of his talents. The extent of his possibilities already seems endless …

'Kylian has the unusual ability to always rise to the occasion,' explains Fanfan Suner, his coach at Bondy. 'Ever since he was a kid, he's always been able to step up at the right time and that hasn't changed since he turned professional.' It was a good job, because since the recent declaration made by his father, he was under close scrutiny. Kylian had no intention of screwing up and he was well aware of the stakes when he was told he had been picked for his second start in the French league a few hours before kick-off for the tenth game of the Ligue 1 season against Montpellier.

'Leonardo Jardim thought it was the right time to give him a second chance,' said an AS Monaco insider. 'The manager was happy with his attitude in the reserve team game the previous weekend and when he came on three days earlier in Moscow it coincided with the hard-fought 1–1 draw on the CSKA pitch in the Champions League. The calendar was starting to look busy and Jardim needed to find alternatives upfront. It was a chance to see what Kylian was made of.'

So here was the number 29, not yet eighteen, walking out onto the pitch of the Stade Louis II to take his position upfront alongside his Colombian captain, Radamel Falcao. 'We were anxious to see what would happen,' remembers Yannick, a fan close to the independent group Ultras Monaco 94. 'We'd been hearing about him for a while and given his performances at the end of the previous season, we didn't understand why he wasn't being given a chance more often. So, of course, when we found out he would be starting, there was a lot of excitement. I kept an eye on him throughout the match and I wasn't disappointed.'

In the eleventh minute, Kylian sounded the revolt after Montpellier opened the scoring. Taking great strides, he went on a run down the left wing. This solo raid ended with a cross to the near post aimed at the head of Bernardo Silva, but it missed by a few inches. Kylian went unrewarded but it was the kind of move that inspired confidence and pointed to what was yet to come. In the twentieth minute, he stepped up for a second time, but his volley was saved at the last minute. In the 35th minute, he would make the difference again and this time his marker was pushed to foul him on the left-hand edge of the area. Penalty! Radamel Falcao wrong-footed the Montpellier keeper to equalise, making it 1–1.

The party was just getting started: only four minutes after the start of the second half, the U19 French international surged towards the far post, quicker yet again than his opposite number, to fire an unstoppable header just past the right post: 'I fought with him in training to get him to use his head sometimes. It's his weakness and I would often tease him about it. It was the right thing to do against Montpellier. It's the mark of a great player,' his coach at the academy, Frédéric Barilaro, would later say. During the last half hour of the game, Kylian was the architect of two more goals: in the 74th minute, he supplied Valère Germain with a flawless cross to make it 4–2, then, two minutes later, provided another ball from the left wing, this time for Thomas Lemar to take advantage. 'Of course, he was the talk of the stands after the game. He'd been directly involved in four of our team's goals. His performance had almost overshadowed the 6–2 spanking we'd just inflicted on Montpellier,' remembers Yannick, the loyal Monaco fan, enthusiastically.

In the corridors of the Louis II, his performance was being dissected by each and every journalist: some liked the variety of his balls, others the way in which his play had focused on his team. Leonardo Jardim was also invited to comment on his young striker's game: 'Mbappé? He's a quality young player. I'm happy with him. Montpellier is an ideal team for him, with plenty of space. It's perfect for the characteristics of his game. He still needs to work hard but we plan to help our young-sters get to the next level.' And what did the man of the moment think? Of course, when the microphones were thrust out towards him and the cameras caught him coming out of the dressing room, Kylian was sport-ing a wide smile that betrayed his relief: 'The manager gave me a chance and I think I managed to grasp it. I'm happy. When I don't play, it's always frustrating because I'm a competitor. But I also play for a great team with great players. I'm here to learn and I spend a lot of time listening to advice from the other players.'

Kylian gave the media a clear and lucid analysis of his match and the delicate situation he had been in since the start of his first professional season. They were discovering another side to the player, that he would become a media star with an unmatched tone to his voice and was someone gifted with a disconcert-ing analytical ability for a seventeen year old: 'I'd had the opportunity to spend time with him for more than a year by then, so I'd got used to it but it's true that many of my colleagues were blown away by the maturity of his comments that night,' said Fabien Pigalle. 'Of course, when you're as good on the pitch as you are in an interview, it plays doubly in your favour.'

With a score of eight out of ten, the *Monaco-Matin* reporter also made Kylian his man of the match ahead of Bernardo Silva and Thomas Lemar: 'He was talent in its purest form during that game. He shone as soon as he found himself back on his favourite side, down the left wing. From then on, he was a threat with every burst of pace.' Two days later, the regional daily even devoted a full page to the young striker, with the headline: 'Mbappé, a thrilling player.' At the end of the article, his former coach, Frédéric Barilaro, was asked two questions: How far can he go? What is his best position? 'We don't know what level he'll get to but he's most comfortable on the left wing, where he can do whatever he likes: cross, shoot or dribble. He can use both feet and his game is more developed than when he started. Kylian has some baffling qualities, particularly when it comes to his ball skills.'

His performance that night had also won over the AS Monaco players. Of course, by then his teammates had had the chance for almost a year to get the measure of the kid's technical skills in training, but this celebration against Montpellier had also proved that the young man had the right mindset and was determined to seize the slightest opportunity to carve out a role for himself in the team's attack. 'We knew he'd been champing at the bit since the start of the season,' said Valère Germain after the match, a player who has since gone to Marseille. 'We hope it's the start of a long run for him. There's going to be plenty of competition upfront and it will make the team better.'

It was obviously still too early for the cards to be completely reshuffled, but 'Razmoket' [Rugrat], as he had been nicknamed by the Monaco dressing room in reference to the cartoon featuring the adventures of some intrepid babies, had undeniably scored points and moved up the hierarchy of the club's strikers. 'His ability to show up at key moments in his career is not all that surprising if you know him a little,' claims a relative. 'He isn't just talented, he also has an incredible self-confidence. How many players would have been paralysed by the pressure and fear of not being able to live up to the statements made publicly? Probably most of them, but not him! He never doubts himself. That's why he's up there with the greats. He has talent, ambition and a fire inside him that he never lets go out.'

That wonderful evening of 21 October 2016 would be followed by a resounding end to the year. The performance had given wings to Kylian, who now soared over any questions asked when he appeared on the team sheet. Between Montpellier and the Christmas break, he racked up four more league starts, one goal against Bastia and two assists. Whenever Jardim brought him on during a game, he was also able to make himself decisive, just as on 5 November against Nancy, when he found an opening with his first touch before providing Diego Carillo with another extremely classy ball to make it 6–0 right at the end of the game. 'It was true that every time he came on, something happened,' said Yannick, the loyal fan. 'Despite the competition upfront, he held his own and was starting to become one of the fans' favourite players.'

His popularity just kept rising. On 14 December, for his club's entry into the League Cup competition, he put on a show against Stade Rennais in the last sixteen: he scored his first goal in the eleventh minute with a burst of speed down the left wing before opening up his right foot perfectly. In the twentieth minute, he helped in a cross deflected by Nabil Dirar at the far post, then distinguished himself for one last time in the 62nd minute on the end of an assist from João Moutinho that he converted with his left foot. Three goals scored in just over an hour earned him yet another record: at just seventeen years, eleven months and 24 days, this time Kylian had become the youngest ever player to score a hat-trick in a Monaco shirt. 'I'd scored twice a lot but never three times,' he said after the match on the touchline. A few days later, he went into more detail during a French television report: 'You always have to send messages in football and yes, I did send a powerful one in the League Cup. Every morning when I get up, I try to be better than I was the day before, to win titles, because that's how you make your mark on history. And that's what I want to do, I want to win titles with AS Monaco.'

During the last match of the year, on 21 December 2016, Kylian achieved his fifth assist in the French league during the 2–1 win over Caen. It was a great way to honour his eighteenth birthday, which he had celebrated the day before, and, most importantly, to confirm how keen he was to play a major role in the second half of AS Monaco's season.

Chapter 11

International

James Robson has been a reporter at the *Manchester Evening News* for more than ten years. He has been following the Citizens since the arrival of Pep Guardiola. Diego Torres is a well-respected writer for the Spanish daily newspaper *El País*. Matthias Dersch writes for the German biweekly *Kicker* and is a regular at the Signal Iduna Park in Dortmund. Guido Vaciago is editor-in-chief of *Tuttosport* and accompanies Juventus across Italy and in Europe. These four journalists came across Kylian during the second half of the 2016–17 season and witnessed his emergence on the international stage.

On Tuesday 21 February, Monaco travelled to the Etihad Stadium to play Manchester City, one of the Champions League favourites, in the last sixteen. 'When the draw was made, we thought we'd done pretty well as, of all the teams to top their groups, Monaco were probably the most beatable on paper,' explains James Robson. 'We knew the team a bit but, to tell the truth, we didn't know anything about Mbappé. During the press conference, Kevin De Bruyne even admitted he'd never heard of him. Personally, if I'd bumped into him in the street, I wouldn't have recognised him! To be fair, he had played very little during the first half of the competition, but when I looked in more detail, I noticed he was in good form.'

After the great performances of late December, Kylian kept up the pace at the start of the year. He scored one goal and provided two assists during two starts in the Coupe de France against AC Ajaccio and FC Chambly. He put his foot on the gas in February, scoring again against Montpellier for his return to the starting eleven in the French league, then coming away from Monaco's 5–0 win over FC Metz with a hat-trick. As a result, Leonardo Jardim gave him his first Champions League start in the first leg of this last sixteen game in an attacking eleven in which he was tasked with supporting Radamel Falcao as centre forward. 'The English journalists didn't necessarily expect to see him start, but the press box was very quickly won over.'

The French striker ran rings around City's defenders in the first half. Nicolás Otamendi and John Stones were flustered by his dribbling and outrun every time he went up through the gears. With a perfect call and a lightning finish, Kylian scored his first Champions League goal in the 41st minute to give his team a 2–1 lead just before the break. 'In the end, Manchester City won 5–3, but that took nothing away from Mbappé's performance. That night we understood why Pep Guardiola had put €40 million on the table the previous summer to try to get a player who was completely unknown in England.'

The Catalan technician had intuition. His impressions were confirmed during the return leg of the last sixteen game two weeks later at the Stade Louis II. Monaco needed something impressive to recover from the two-goal deficit and Kylian took charge of giving his team the best possible start by opening the scoring in the eighth minute on the end of a powerful cross in front of goal from Bernardo Silva. 'He'd already gone down in history in the first leg by becoming the second youngest French player to score in the Champions League [behind Karim Benzema] and now he'd done it again in this crucial game. All the English press already had him down as the new Thierry Henry.' In the 29th minute, Kylian was the instigator of Monaco's second goal: although this time he neither scored the goal nor provided the assist, he did initiate the frenetic counter-attack concluded by a winning shot from the inside of Fabinho's foot. Monaco qualified for the quarter-finals beating Manchester City 3–1: 'Of course, he didn't knock City out single-handedly, but as far as I was concerned, he was the best player across both games,' concluded James Robson.

And, because good news never comes on its own, the day after Kylian's exploits against the Sky Blues, he learned of his first call-up for the France A team. He hadn't even needed to take the Under 21s route; here he was picked directly by the France manager Didier Deschamps for two important games scheduled for the end of March: a qualifying game for the 2018 World Cup and a blue-riband friendly at the Stade de France in Saint-Denis against Spain. Like everyone else, Diego Torres, an editor at *El País*, found out about Kylian's debut for Les Bleus via social media: his arrival at the Clairefontaine training centre in his mother, Fayza's, car and his initiation during the first team meal. 'News of his performances against Manchester City had reverberated as far as Spain,' said the journalist, who was also following Real Madrid. 'Some experts were saying he had invented things only Maradona had ever done before. They were unanimously adamant that they hadn't seen such a talented youngster in nearly 30 years.'

After winning his first cap on 25 March by coming on for Dimitri Payet in the 78th minute of the 3–1 win over Luxembourg, Kylian was in the starting eleven three days later against Spain at the Stade de France. This gala match was clearly an international baptism of fire. With France taking on the 2010 world champions, the game was a tantalising prospect and Kylian had the opportunity to show what he could do very close to home, in front of his family and friends. The result was not up to his expectations: 'France focused solely on defending, playing a game that didn't favour talented players and logically they lost 2–0 to the Roja. But amid the collective disaster, Mbappé was the only player to hold his own during the 60 minutes he spent on the pitch. Every time he touched the ball, something happened. He confirmed what I'd said about him in an article entitled "The Gazelle and the Panther." In my opinion, he was the perfect modern striker because he was the only one who combined, from the outset, the technique of Zidane and Benzema with the agility and speed of Thierry Henry and Samuel Eto'o. The comparison may have been daring but it soon became clear we were dealing with an exceptional player.'

A two-time scorer against Manchester City and looking his best in a France shirt, Kylian continued his irresistible rise in the Champions League quarter-finals. This time, it was the turn of Germany to fall under the spell of the French prodigy. Against the Borussia Dortmund of his friend Ousmane Dembélé, he gave a consummate performance on 12 April 2017 in the first leg played at the Signal Iduna Park. Against the 'yellow wall', as the imposing Borussia kop is known, he scored in both halves to help Monaco to a 3–2 win. Unfortunately, Kylian's first European 'double' would go unnoticed due to a tragic event: the day before, as it was leaving the hotel for the stadium, the Borussia team bus had fallen victim to a bomb attack resulting in two minor injuries, including one to the Spanish player, Marc Bartra, whose wrist was wounded. A club supporter, a German–Russian in his late twenties, had detonated three explosive devices as the bus went past: 'We came close to disaster that night,' remembers the *Kicker* journalist, Matthias Dersch, with emotion in his voice. 'The match was postponed until the following day, but the minds of the players, fans and journalists were all still elsewhere. We'd come very close to a national disaster!'

Kylian would pay tribute to his opponents after the game: 'Of course, we were delighted to have landed an important blow, but mostly we were really affected by what had happened. After the explosion, I immediately called Ousmane Dembélé and told him we were all with him, Bartra and all the Dortmund players.'

These comments were particularly appreciated by the Borussia fans and would do much to increase his popularity. The German public were becoming acquainted with an eighteen-year-old boy of surprising maturity and unlimited talent: 'At the time, we weren't necessarily paying attention, but watching the game back later we realised the measure of his performance,' said Matthias Dersch. 'He'd done everything in that first match: won a penalty [missed by Fabinho], tried his luck a number of times and found his way through twice. For the first goal, which he scored with his knee, he was offside, but for the second he did something fantastic. He picked up the ball, shook off the defenders and took on Bürki with incredible confidence. Despite his young age, he never panicked, took his time to get into the best position and curled the ball with his right foot past the keeper and under the bar. It was a goal worthy of some of the greatest players.'

To celebrate his two goals, Kylian set off on an endless slide and, for the first time, performed the celebration that would be beamed around the world. Full of confidence, with his arms crossed and his chest and head held high. The pose would become the signature of his greatest exploits. 'It came out of nothing, I was playing PlayStation with my little brother. He scored a goal and celebrated by doing this [crossing his arms]. Five minutes later, he stopped and said to me: "Kylian, you could do that in a match." I asked him: "Do you want me to do it? Okay, I'll do it." So it happened in Dortmund and I did it. He was happy. I told him: "Now I've stolen it, it's mine!"' Kylian would tell the BeIN Sports microphones.

A week later, history would repeat itself in the quarter-final return leg. Barely three minutes had been played at the Louis II when the new French phenomenon was already on the lookout to convert a powerful shot from Benjamin Mendy that was fumbled by Bürki. Same cause, same effect: the kid from Bondy opened the scoring and remembered his celebration, with his arms crossed over his chest and a stare on his face. Monaco eventually won 3–1 thanks to two other goals scored by Falcao and Valère Germain.

His first European adventure would come to an end in early May in Turin. Kylian would not see the Millennium Stadium in Cardiff, where the Real Madrid of his idol Cristiano Ronaldo would be crowned Champions League winners for the twelfth time in the club's history on 3 June. He would, however, do every-thing possible to take his club to the final, but it would turn out not to be enough to overcome Juventus. 'After everything we'd already heard and read about him, the Italians were keen to see what he could do,' said the *Tuttosport* journalist, Guido Vaciago. The opportunity presented itself on 3 May 2017. As he came out onto the pitch, Kylian was accompanied by his younger brother Ethan, appointed a 'hand-holder' mascot for the first leg of the semi-final in the principality. He started with a few moves: a soft header in the thirteenth minute, then another shot with his inside foot, parried by Buffon, in the sixteenth minute. That was almost it. This time, Kylian remained silent, unlike Gonzalo Higuaín, who scored twice: 'In the first leg, I thought Mbappé was a little inhibited by the stakes, probably a bit in awe at facing a Juve team that had just knocked out Barcelona. But during the return leg, he was back to what had done so much damage at Manchester City and Dortmund. He really let himself go …'

After the 2–0 defeat in front of their own fans, Monaco had nothing left to lose: 'Yes, Juve did win again, but Jardim's players caused the Bianconeri huge problems. Mbappé brought the score line back to 2–1 by skimming the near post just in front of Buffon. But what I remember most was that he was the striker who had posed the biggest problems to our defence throughout the competition. Barzagli, who is famous in Serie A and in Europe for his pace, suffered like never before.'

His well-used right foot tricked Gigi Buffon in the 69th minute to score what would be his sixth and last goal in the 2016–17 Champions League campaign. As the final whistle blew, Kylian was obviously disappointed to see a first European final be taken from under his nose.

But the wonderful embrace with the veteran Italian goalkeeper at the end of the game spoke volumes: in just a few months, he had forged a name and a reputation on the international stage. 'We may have been knocked out but we can hold our heads up high,' said Kylian in the corridors of the Allianz Stadium. 'We've had a good run, we started in the preliminaries and climbed up through the ranks with all our strength and our attacking game, but we've also managed to answer a few questions and we don't have too many regrets about this European campaign. Rubbing shoulders with the very best is the best way to make progress. We learned a lot today, I learned a lot. And we'll try to come back next season with better weapons.'

Just a few metres away, the journalist Guido Vaciago

was collecting Italian impressions. 'The players and staff were all relieved by this qualification, but they were also appreciative of Mbappé's performance. I remember bumping into the sporting director, Giuseppe Marotta, near the dressing rooms and I said to him, laughing: "You need to buy Mbappé!" He fired right back: "Mbappé? We could have had him for next to nothing a couple of years ago. Now it's too late. All the big clubs are after him. Now he's a player with an international reputation."'

Chapter 12

A champion already

Elimination at the hands of Juventus would eventually turn out to be a blessing in disguise. It did much to heighten Monegasque ambitions. 'The Champions League run had bonded the squad together and allowed Kylian to break through,' said a former player and regular in the stands at the Louis II. 'Now they only had one goal in mind: the French league title.'

At the beginning of May, in the last few weeks of the season, AS Monaco were in an ideal position ahead of Paris Saint-Germain. Jardim's players had had a firm grip on the top of Ligue 1 since re-claiming their spot in mid-January after a big 4–1 win at Marseille. 'Kylian only played very briefly that night, but he soon caught up and went on to play a decisive role in all competitions,' the former player continued.

After clicking in the Champions League in Manchester, Kylian succeeded in stringing matches and performances together: on 25 February at Guingamp, he won a penalty shortly after coming on in the 2–1 win.

On 1 March, at the Stade Vélodrome in the last

sixteen of the Coupe de France, he scored once and provided Benjamin Mendy with an assist for a 4–3 win after extra time at Olympique de Marseille's ground.

On 5 March, he scored two goals at home against FC Nantes. The following day, the sports newspaper *L'Équipe* put him on its front page for the first time with the headline 'The Magician'. 'He was really starting to be talked about on all media fronts,' remembers Fabien Pigalle from *Monaco-Matin*. 'His every performance was picked apart and curiosity had given way to fear on the part of his opponents.'

As well as respect. After another goal that broke the deadlock against Bordeaux on 11 March, Kylian raised the roof at the stadium in Caen the following weekend. 'He did everything in that game: he opened the scoring shortly after beating two defenders and the keeper with disconcerting ease, won a penalty after amazing everyone with his pace and scored for a second time with his head on the end of a cross from João Moutinho. It was a top-flight performance that came just after his display against Manchester City and the announcement of his first call-up for the France team.' In the 88th minute, Kylian received a standing ovation from the fans at the Stade Michel d'Ornano as he left the pitch: 'He had just heaped misery on the local team and their fans were giving him a standing ovation! I'd never seen that before other than on TV for big stars. He was only eighteen and he was already winning over the hearts of his opponents' supporters. Although you do have to remember that he had history with Caen, whom he'd almost signed for when he was twelve or thirteen.'

Kylian had become an indispensable player in Jardim's team and one of the darlings of the dressing room: 'His goals obviously helped him integrate. He was very close to Benjamin Mendy, who nicknamed him "Razmoket" in reference to the American *Rugrats* cartoon.' Kylian showed off how happy he was on social media spontaneously with comical scenes of squad life: he filmed Bernardo Silva in his underwear in the canteen, joked around like a kid at the pool with Thomas Lemar and even tried his hand at being a chef for Benjamin Mendy. 'He was at ease with the professional group, to which he brought a freshness. But he didn't forget his friends from the academy either and would sometimes spend the night at the training centre when his parents were away from the Cap d'Ail apartment. To avoid temptation,' said a former associate. 'As he didn't have his driving licence yet his mother would take him to training in an old saloon that was hardly a limousine.'

'As soon as he'd spoken to the press, he would look for Fayza and Ethan after home games to join them as soon as possible. You could see he was very close to his little brother, who would often appear on his social media accounts,' says *Fast Foot* journalist Damien Chedeville. 'You could also see that he didn't go over the top with fashion; he was always wearing a tracksuit, there was no bling. He'd never been seen in nightclubs, unlike the club's other young players of the same age. It didn't interest him. He was about family and was 100 per cent focused on his objectives.'

Kylian was concentrating on the end of the season and the first important game scheduled for 1 April 2017 in Lyon, where the final of the League Cup was to be played for the first time. It promised to be a mouth-watering encounter that would pit the two top teams in France at that time against one another, AS Monaco and Paris Saint-Germain. 'Unai Emery's men had gone out of the Champions League with a humiliating loss to Barcelona [a 6–1 defeat in the last sixteen second leg game on 8 March] and as they sensed that the French title was slipping away from them, the domestic cups were the only way to save their season. The match therefore represented much more than just a League Cup final. It was an opportunity for them to go up in the esteem of their supporters and to show that PSG was still the number one club in the country,' said a journalist. The Paris team's desire and determination made the difference and AS Monaco were swept away on that spring evening, suffering a stinging 4–1 defeat at the hands of Cavani and Di María, despite a stunning equaliser from Thomas Lemar on the half hour. Like most of his teammates, the final completely passed Kylian by.

'It's true that he hardly put in an appearance. It's unusual for him to be absent like that in such an important game,' analysed a relative. It must be said that PSG's central defence did not give him any gifts, as the goalkeeper Danijel Subašić would later tell the Croatian newspaper, *24sata*: 'Thiago Silva was on him from the first minute to the last. He really went in on him hard. You could see he wanted to destroy his confidence. After the game, in the dressing room, Mbappé was really sad, he was on the verge of tears, very emotional and I was sorry to see him in that state. I consoled him and told him it was normal because he'd showed everyone how good he was and that it would keep happening.'

With his self-confidence dented and disappointed at not being able to secure a first professional title, Kylian responded like a champion in the weeks to come: he scored twice against Lyon and Toulouse in two decisive Ligue 1 wins in April. In May, he failed to score at Nancy or Lille, but still stood out, with an assist for Lemar in Lorraine and two key moves against Lille at the Louis II, including another run at goal. At the end of the first half, Kylian strung together a world-class sequence: after picking up the ball deep on the right wing, he went round a defender and got the ball back before literally dancing around his opponent, wrong-footing him with feints, step-overs and turns. The victim was powerless in the face of so much pace and technique. And, once he had had his fun, the number 29 shook off his marker to serve up the ball on a plate for Bernardo Silva. 'That move against Lille was reminiscent of Brazilian Ronaldo's dribbling. R9, not CR7. It was phenomenal!' enthused a Monegasque journalist.

On 15 May, the hitch in the League Cup final was forgotten once and for all: Kylian was unsurprisingly voted the best Under 21 player in Ligue 1. At the traditional ceremony, he came in ahead of his teammate Thomas Lemar, Adrien Rabiot from PSG and Wylan Cyprien from Nice. 'I'm delighted to win this prize. It's really flattering to see my hard work rewarded and it's another reason to keep working and to get to the highest possible level,' said the successor to Ousmane Dembélé during an interview in a live link-up with the principality. Like his teammates, Kylian had not been allowed to make the journey to Paris to receive his trophy as the season was not quite over. AS Monaco had a late-night game two days later at the Louis II that would turn out to be decisive in the title race.

By the time they played host to AS Saint-Etienne on 17 May, Jardim's team only needed a draw to secure the club's eighth French league title. Naturally, Kylian's teammates did not miss out on the opportunity and gave the fans, who came in their numbers for once, a treat. The former Bondy player was the trigger once again: in the nineteenth minute, he was put through down the middle by Radamel Falcao, about 30 yards from goal.

His pace allowed him to shake off his two pursuers in a few strides and to take out the AS Saint-Étienne goalkeeper with baffling ease. He started with a dummy to bring the goalkeeper to ground before calmly despatching the ball into the open goal. It had all taken a matter of seconds. And with bags of style. One–nil. Kylian had coolly scored his 26th and last goal of a season that had also allowed him to deliver fourteen assists. Statistics worthy of the greatest strikers in Europe and almost unheard of for an eighteen-year-old player who had barely been used during the first six months of the season.

Shortly afterwards, Monaco scored a second time through Valère Germain. But by then it was incidental. The scenes of joy that followed the final whistle shortly before 11pm would go down in history. On the pitch, in the dressing rooms and in the press room, the new champions swept everything before them. The excitement was in keeping with the feat that brought an end to Paris Saint-Germain's four-year unbroken reign over French football: 'It was madness,' said a journalist sent to the principality for the event. 'Jardim's press conference was cut short by the arrival of about ten players. Benjamin Mendy was really excited. They were singing and dancing like kids! Kylian was happy but he was a little more reserved. He was almost the only one who wasn't taking selfies. It was as if he wanted to enjoy the moment quietly; he kept his happiness inside.'

'Everyone has their own way of celebrating. I wanted to look out at the stadium. The club had put on an amazing party with fireworks. The stadium was full and I didn't see the point in having my phone,' he would tell TF1. Nor did Kylian think it was necessary to set off on a jaunt with his teammates to celebrate the win at a nightclub: 'It tells you a bit more about him as a person and his strength of character,' said a club insider. 'He didn't go out partying with his teammates, but, two days later, he was in Seine-Saint-Denis with Vice President Vadim Vasilyev to present the French champions' trophy to the inhabitants of Bondy. It showed his attachment to his hometown and his first club, but also the dimension he'd taken on in the AS Monaco team. He wasn't their great young hopeful any more but he'd become the club's star. As proof, the directors would certainly never have allowed the defender Andrea Raggi to present the trophy back at home in Italy.'

Chapter 13

The saga of the summer

'Seriously, I don't know. I spoke to the vice president and set myself the goal of finishing the season well and winning the title. We put everything else aside. My priority was to win something at the club where I trained. I put all the ingredients into it to make it happen. I put everything to do with rumours and transfer talk away in a box and we'll see. When am I going to open the box again? After I've played for the France team.'

Only four days had passed since the French title had been decided and Kylian was already having to answer the question of the summer: where would he play next season? On Sunday 21 May, he was a special guest on *Telefoot*, filmed on the pitch at the Stade Louis II, during which he gave a good account of himself and managed to postpone any decision until after the games he was due to play for the national team in the first two weeks in June. Alongside him on the makeshift TV set was Vadim Vasilyev, Vice President of AS Monaco, who promised: 'We're going to do everything we can to keep him.'

Prince Albert II also hoped he would stay in Monaco: 'He wants to stay. And I don't think I'm revealing any secrets by saying that his father also wants him to stay. There might be some last-minute changes I'm not aware of,' the Monegasque head of state told the Canal+ microphones, 'but for the time being he will still be at AS Monaco next year.' These reassuring declarations came in the face of a flurry of front pages (see *Marca*, which described Kylian as '*La Joja del mercado*'), rumours and multimillion euro offers. It was nothing new: Kylian had been attracting the interest of big European clubs since he was fourteen, but now, after making his mark on the Champions League at Manchester City, there were plenty who wasted no time offering lorryloads of money to secure the services of the new phenomenon of European football. Florentino Pérez – the president of Real Madrid, who had seen Kylian in action against Guardiola's City in the UCL last sixteen and decided he would be the next *galáctico* – was one of these. He did not think twice about getting out his wallet to bring him to the Bernabéu. According to *Marca*, Mbappé had already expressed an interest: 'He wants to play in Madrid and told the club's representatives so when they contacted his entourage,' the Spanish newspaper claimed on 5 May. The deal was expected to be done for a figure in the region of €100 million.

But Real were not the only ones to get involved.

In early May, the *Guardian* reported that Manchester United had offered £72 million for Mbappé. It wrote that José Mourinho, the Red Devils' Portuguese manager, had made the Parisian eighteen year old the number one target on his shopping list. It was a shame – according to the British press at least – that AS Monaco had rejected the offer. The French press claimed that Real Madrid's offer of €130 million had also been returned to sender. It was a huge sum of money, a record amount: it exceeded the figure paid by United to Juventus for Paul Pogba in 2016 and the €100 million Real Madrid had paid Tottenham for Gareth Bale in 2013.

But the principality club did not need to sell, or at least so they said, and they wanted to hold on to their star for one more season, hoping that the price would rise even higher. A bidding war for the red-and-white's number 29 began among the continent's biggest names. It was not only Florentino and the Special One who were interested in the Petit Prince; Mbappé topped the wish lists of Juventus, Manchester City, Arsenal, Liverpool and PSG, to name but a few. Take the 'Old Lady': the Bianconeri's directors, with the Champions League semi-final fresh in their minds, had met with Monaco, according to *Tuttosport*, to talk about transfers and 'the new Thierry Henry' in particular. Take Paris Saint-Germain: Antero Henrique, the former vice president of FC Porto who had just been appointed sporting director at PSG, met Wilfrid in Bondy to discuss the club's plans for his son. According to *L'Équipe*, a meeting had taken place in Paris between Nasser Al-Khelaifi, the club president, and the Mbappé family, a cordial meeting that had ended without a decision being made.

At this point in the story, Kylian seemed determined to stay at Monaco, obviously after adjusting the details of his contract that was due to expire in 2019. Whatever the case, he already had commitments with Les Bleus. These began in Rennes on 2 June, with a friendly against Paraguay. Three days earlier, Kylian had been forced, yet again, to talk about his future in a press conference at Clairefontaine. 'If you leave Monaco, is there a risk you'll get less time on the pitch?', they asked him. The following answer came from a boy clearly tired of having to repeat the same thing: 'Why would I get less time on the pitch? That doesn't frighten me about leaving. But I have time to think about it. I'm focusing on this international call-up before anything else. There's plenty of time to think about all that. We have three important games to play and I'll take stock after that.' He added that the opinion of Didier Deschamps on the transfer mattered but that 'he would not guide my choice.' He also talked at length about Zidane: 'He made me dream when he was a player, still makes me dream when I come across clips of him. Being a manager is completely different. He's a great coach who's started with some fantastic results and is developing.'

In some quarters of the French media, this statement was interpreted as the door closing on Real Madrid's advances.

On 2 June, Mbappé did not take to the pitch against Paraguay because he was carrying a knock to the thigh. Didier Deschamps wanted to protect him ahead of the other games. He even forbade him from touching the ball, although the scallywag from Bondy did not do as he was told.

France beat Paraguay 5–0 at Roazhon Park. It was a useful warm-up before the match that counted, a qualifier for the 2018 World Cup against Sweden. It was a miserable night for Les Bleus at Solna on 9 June. In the 94th minute, a goal from the Toulouse player Ola Toivonen gave the Swedes a 2–1 win after a blatant mistake from Hugo Lloris. France suffered their first defeat and relinquished their place at the top of World Cup qualifying group A to the team in yellow and blue. What about Kylian? He came on for a disappointing Griezmann in the 76th minute and had little chance to show what he was made of.

On 13 June, it was the turn of England in a top-flight friendly: France had not beaten the English since 2010. It was an important test game after the blow in Sweden. The match was played in Paris, at the Stade de France. Kylian Mbappé Lottin was in the starting eleven for the first time. He was partnered with Olivier Giroud upfront. Before the kick-off, the English and French fans sang along to *Don't Look Back in Anger*, played by a Republican Guard on an electric guitar in the middle of the pitch. It was a tribute to the victims of the recent terrorist attacks in Manchester and London. When the final whistle was blown by Davide Massa, the match referee, the result was 3–2 to France.

Praise was heaped by both the French and British press on Mbappé, Ousmane Dembélé and Paul Pogba. They were unanimous. This was the judgement of *Le Figaro*: 'Like Dembélé, the Monaco player caught fire as soon as he got possession of the ball. His movements are perfectly measured. Everything is devised to hurt the opponent and never to play to the gallery. Every provocation is a feast for the eyes and an ordeal for the defenders. He hit the bar (71) and supplied Dembélé with an assist (78). He needs to sharpen his killer instinct but must hold on to his insouciance at all costs. This kid is a real gem.' His performance was marked seven out of ten. Those at the BBC were even more generous. They gave him an eight out of ten and voiced plenty of positive comments: 'Pace, trickery, industry. You can see why the exciting Monaco youngster has been linked with a big-money move. Caused the England backline all sorts of problems, but struck the crossbar when he should have scored into a gaping net.' It's hard to imagine a more enthusiastic assessment.

What did Kylian think of the game and of his season as a whole? 'Let's say that it's ended well and could have started better. I wanted to play and succeed. I've managed to do that at the end but I have to do it over the course of a whole year.' Obviously, the by now usual question about his future came from the journalists stationed in the corridors of the Stade de France: 'Hang on, I've just come off the pitch. I'm going to go away with my family for the next few days and will think about what's going to happen,' he smiled and went to leave, but someone insisted and tried again, 'Are you going to pick a club?' 'Yes, and talk to my club as well, of course. I'm under contract, I'm not free.'

For Kylian it was time to jet off on holiday. The following day he posted a photograph on Twitter: 'Holiday Attitude. With big brother @JiresKembo_'. The surprise was that the Petit Prince was sporting a platinum blonde hairdo like Kembo.

The pictures that followed came from a yacht moored in Spanish waters off Mallorca. The idea was total relaxation with the family. But unfortunately his holiday would not be all that peaceful. There was a future to be decided. There were different opinions to be heard and the various offers made by the richest clubs in the world to be considered. They needed to be carefully weighed up, evaluated and analysed with the help of his parents, but the last word would be Kylian's. So between swims in the sea, the boy from Bondy had more conversations with Vasilyev to make sure of Monaco's intentions and took a phone call from

Zinedine Zidane. The coach of the Merengues, who was just back from a holiday of his own in Italy, called the Monaco striker to convince him to pack his bags and fly to Madrid. This was the so-called 'secret conversation' revealed by *L'Équipe* on its front page on 23 June and later denied by an Mbappé family insider.

What could Zizou have said to Kylian? Les Bleus' former number 10 assuaged the talented young player's fears about ending up on the bench, about not having enough pitch time, in short of not making progress as a footballer. He promised Kylian he would get time on the pitch, that the three-pronged 'BBC' attack (Bale, Benzema, Cristiano Ronaldo) was not set in stone and that if Bale returned to his beloved United Kingdom, as was rumoured, Kylian would have a spot in the starting eleven or his place in the Madrid attacking rotation would be guaranteed. That was not all: the manager promised the French phenomenon that, at Madrid, he would become the worldwide star he dreamt of being.

These were powerful arguments that seemed to spark enthusiasm in the young man from Bondy. But there was time left to choose and plenty of other important conversations planned. Such as the one with Unai Emery. The Basque manager reflected on Kylian on 8 June during a round table at the Bilbao International Football Summit. 'When they talk about Mbappé here in Spain, they talk about Real Madrid and Barcelona. But I'm in Paris, at PSG. As far as I'm concerned, what could be better than being able to represent a French team? If it's true that he's going to become one of the icons of world football, he should be in Paris, with all due respect to Monaco. He's from Paris, his family are in Paris. What could be better for France, for PSG, than for there to be a union, a communion between the player and his city?' Not even a month later the coach was in Bondy. He met Kylian for the first time, talked about his future and a role for him in the starting eleven at the Paris club. But for the Mbappés, PSG were the third possible choice behind Monaco and Real Madrid. A house move confirmed Kylian's wish to stay at the Monaco club. He left the apartment where he had lived with Fayza for a house in the hills above Cap d'Ail, two doors up from where James Rodríguez had lived. The idea was that after so much back and forth between Bondy and Monaco, the whole Mbappé family would be able to live quietly in the large house with sea views that had previously been occupied by his friend Benjamin Mendy.

On Monday 10 July, after his holidays in Spain and Greece, Kylian arrived at La Turbie for the usual medical and some light training overseen by Leonardo Jardim. On Thursday 13 July, the Monegasque squad arrived in Saillon in the Swiss canton of Valais for a training camp that would last until 19 July. Mbappé was the star; there was a crowd waiting for him at the end of every training session, but it was not only the fans who were keen to get a selfie with the Petit Prince, a multitude of journalists were also in attendance. The question was repeated *ad nauseam*: are you going to stay at Monaco despite the offers made by Real, Manchester City and PSG? The Madrid-based sports daily *AS* reported the phenomenon's simple response: 'I don't know,' the same thing he had said a month earlier. Even so, these three words would still be enough to fan the flames of another instalment of the summer saga. Special correspondents, journalists and pundits would try to find good reasons for the boy to choose to stay at Monaco or set off for distant shores. Once again Prince Albert II, interviewed by *L'Équipe* on 12 July, would also say his piece: 'Talks are under way that lead me to think he will still be at Monaco next season. The discussions are about an increase in his salary. But I think he has understood, as has his father, that it is not yet in his interest to go to a big club, where he's not certain of getting into the first team. Even if Zidane has said he would get playing time at Real Madrid.'

One wonders if the statements made by the prince were those of someone aware of the facts or simply the wishes of a fan … The fact was that many, both fans and otherwise, were in agreement with His Serene Highness and hoped that quick negotiations would lead to a contract extension, putting an end to the affair that had already dragged on for too long. After all, Kylian's place in the starting eleven would be almost unquestionable;

he would inherit the number 10 from Bernardo Silva, who had gone to Manchester City, could count on a monthly salary of €700,000 and would avoid the risk of spending too much time on the bench in a World Cup year.

The *coup de théâtre* came on 14 July, Bastille Day. In his room at the Hôtel des Bains de Saillon, Kylian recorded a video message that he posted on Twitter at 9.46pm, captioned '*Grande annonce*' (Big announcement). Fans in France and Spain pricked up their ears, not to mention journalists from all over the world. He had finally decided if he was staying or going, and if so where. With a serious face and a solemn tone worthy of an important occasion, Mbappé says:

'Hello everyone, it's me. As you know, my name has recently been linked to lots of different things. There have been lots of rumours. I think it's important for me to update you and give you this information. I've thought about it a lot with my family. We've weighed up the pros and cons. We've reached a decision, which is that … this year … from now on … I'm going to play …,' Kylian stops to catch his breath. The suspense hits its peak. He reaches down and comes back up to the camera holding a pair of football boots. And laughing like crazy, he exclaims: 'In Mercurial Vapors!' It was a publicity stunt for Nike, with whom Mbappé had just renewed his contract, adding a few zeros. It was a great way of creating a buzz, but not everyone liked it. Kylian later justified it as a joke in a second video: 'They asked me to do it, I thought it would be fun and it didn't hurt anyone.'

On 20 July, AS Monaco saw red. In an official statement, they took issue with the European clubs that had 'contacted Kylian Mbappé [and his entourage] without authorisation from the club'. They threatened to ask the French governing body and FIFA to issue disciplinary sanctions towards clubs that contravened the rules. According to some, it was a message addressed to PSG, Real Madrid and Arsenal. A strong signal, others interpreted, that the principality club wanted to hold on tight to French football's new young star.

But that was not quite how things were. Monaco were playing at two tables. On the one hand, they claimed they wanted to extend the boy from Bondy's contract; on the other, they were negotiating his sale to Real Madrid. In short, the statement seemed like a warning not necessarily addressed to the Casa Bianca, but to City, who, according to the British media, were getting ready to put £143 million on the table. Pep Guardiola, the Catalan manager, had reportedly had several telephone conversations with Kylian and his father. He was said to have offered Kylian the chance to be in the Sky Blues' first team, talked about his footballing philosophy and tactics, and to have tried to convince him to take the route chosen by some of his Monaco teammates.

But negotiations with Los Blancos were already advanced. A meeting in mid-July between Florentino Pérez and José Ángel Sánchez on one side and Dmitry Rybolovlev on the other was thought to have established the terms of a possible agreement. On 26 July, *Marca* took aim on its front page: 'Agreement in principle for Mbappé: 180 million. The Frenchman could become the most expensive signing in the history of football.' The paper went on to say the following in the two pages dedicated exclusively to the story: 'Once the remaining details have been worked out, the young French player will sign for six seasons, during each of which he will earn €7 million. The intention on all sides [Madrid and the striker himself] is that he will join up with the team currently on tour in the United States within the next few days.'

It was also claimed that Madrid had considered closing the deal but leaving Mbappé at Monaco for one more season, an option the principality club was thought to favour. But, still according to *Marca*, after several meetings with Zidane and one with Florentino Pérez in Paris, the player had decided he didn't want to drag things out and that despite competition from the 'BBC' he felt capable of carving out a place for himself in the Real Madrid starting eleven.

'I can assure you that there is no agreement with Real Madrid or any other club.' The denial from Vadim Vasilyev came later that same day. The vice president of

AS Monaco confirmed he had received requests from all sides but reiterated that there were no pre-agreements.

Monaco may have been talking but the Mbappé clan remained silent.

Kylian did his talking on the pitch, on 29 July at the Stade Ibn Batouta in Tangier during the Champions Trophy 2017. Monaco, champions of Ligue 1, played Paris Saint-Germain, winners of the Coupe de France. Mbappé was partnered in attack by the captain Radamel Falcao. The boy was brilliant in the first half. He had a goal disallowed for offside, was on target with a shot saved by the defender Marquinhos and showed pace and dribbling. In the second half, when the Monegasques gradually lost control of the ball, he fell away and was replaced by Carrillo. PSG celebrated their fifth title in the 94th minute. The Man of the Match was Dani Alves; Paris's newly purchased Brazilian left his mark on the game with a great goal from a free-kick and an assist for Adrien Rabiot to make it 2–1.

On 3 August, PSG officially announced the signing of Neymar Junior. It was the most expensive transfer in footballing history: €222 million. The Brazilian had signed a contract until 30 June 2022. He would earn something close to €36 million a year. It brought an end to an incredible story over which rivers of ink had been spilled and hours and hours of comment had been made on television and websites all over the world. It had been a brief but intense whirlwind that had eclipsed the Mbappé deal. Now that Barcelona's former number 11 had arrived at the court of Nasser Al-Khelaifi, everything seemed clear to the Spanish media. PSG were now out of the running for Mbappé; Manchester City and Arsenal had given up … it was only a matter of days before the young French star would sign for Madrid.

The 2017–18 Ligue 1 season began on 4 August. The Monaco team was conspicuous by its absences. Mendy and Bernardo Silva had gone to City, Babayoko to Chelsea, Germain to Marseille, Diallo to Mainz, Jean to Toulouse and Dirar to Fenerbahce. The standouts among the new arrivals were Youri Tielemans, the young Belgian midfielder who had cost €25 million, and Terence Kongolo, the Dutch defender formerly at Feyenoord. The first test of the league season came against Toulouse, a game that finished 3–2 in favour of the home team, Monaco. Wearing the number 10 shirt, Mbappé left the pitch in the 74th minute after taking a hefty blow to his left knee. It was certainly a scare but one that turned out to be nothing serious. The next day, Kylian was in Manchester for a sponsor event. He had a selfie with Sané, while Mendy, his old friend, joked about the fact that Kylian might choose Guardiola's Citizens. Meanwhile, in France, Vasilyev gave every assurance that Mbappé 'has never expressed a desire to leave. We are still in talks with him. It's not just a question of money, it's more complicated than that. The player has to weigh things up on the football-ing front. He's thinking about it at the moment and that's completely normal.'

In Spain, things became even more involved. According to the Madrid press, Monaco wanted more money, a bonus of €25 million if Mbappé won the Ballon d'Or while playing for Real. But it was more than simply a financial question; there was the fact that Zidane was not keen to handle four strikers of the cali-bre of Cristiano Ronaldo, Gareth Bale, Karim Benzema and Kylian Mbappé. It was a situation that could lead to problems and conflict in the dressing room. It was true that Alvaro Morata had gone to Chelsea, but the situation was still complicated. In other words, Zizou could only see a deal with Mbappé working if Bale left for the Premier League.

The tenth of August: two sources on either side of the Pyrenees were in agreement. 'Unless the situation changes, we can confirm that @KMbappe is coming to Paris,' announced *ParisUnited*, a website from the French capital that always has its ear to the ground. *Marca* confirmed: 'The impossible is about to happen. Kylian Mbappé will become a PSG player. Case closed.'

What happened? How could things have changed so quickly? Jean-François 'Fanfan' Suner, a family friend and one of Kylian's first coaches back in Bondy, explains: 'When he found out Monaco had agreed terms with Real behind his back, he wasn't happy at all. So he decided to leave, but to go where HE wanted to go. He didn't want to take anyone for a ride so he chose Paris as he thought that was the only way to guarantee playing time. First and foremost, the kid loves to play. He wasn't sure Real could promise he would get to play in the Clásico. As they hadn't managed to sell Bale, he didn't want to risk being on the bench. He chose PSG and waited for the Paris team to come to an agreement with Monaco. Although the deal was done at the end of August, Kylian had decided about ten days earlier that he would join PSG.' It would take 21 days before the signing finally became official. Three difficult weeks for Kylian and the Mbappé family.

Chapter 14

31 August 2017

The game had been over for a while. The French team had beaten the Netherlands 4–0. And, thanks to Bulgaria's daring victory over Sweden (3–2), Les Bleus were on top of Group A and had qualification for the 2018 Russia World Cup in their sights. In the belly of the Stade de France, the TV, radio and print media tribes were waiting. Almost everyone had gone through the mixed zone apart from Thomas Lemar, who had been held back by anti-doping control. But he was not the one the journalists were waiting for. Then, shortly after midnight, shortly after the end of the summer transfer window, Kylian, the most hotly anticipated player, appeared in front of the savage hordes. Wearing a blue French national team t-shirt, flip-flops and a smile on his lips, Kylian Mbappé offered himself up to the media. Microphones appeared out of nowhere and questions came from all sides.

*'With your first goal for France and the official
announcement of your signing for PSG, has it been a dream
night for you?'*

'It's been a great day, a great signing, a great win and
a goal. A dream day? Yes, almost. I'm not really sure
what a typical dream day is like but it's been a fantastic
day. We had an amazing match from start to finish,
played on our own terms. I think the fans enjoyed it
and so did we. Everyone's happy today. We're proud of
being able to put in a performance like that. We gave
a good account of ourselves against a great team today.
We hope we can continue in the same way.'

'Why did you decide to join Paris Saint-Germain?'

'It's official. I'm delighted to be joining such a great
club. It's the ideal place for me to make progress and
continue learning at the highest level. I'm going to
be surrounded by some great players, most of whom
have won everything at domestic level and some even
at European level, so I've got lots to learn and everything to prove.'

*'The biggest clubs in Europe were after you. When did you
pick PSG?'*

'Several weeks ago. Why PSG? Because that was
where I thought I would make the most progress,
while playing as much as possible. That was my main
requirement.'

'OK. That's enough, thank you.' Philippe Tournon, the France team's press officer, had to intervene. He put his arm around the boy's shoulders and led him away. On this important day, 31 August 2017, there would never be an end to the journalists' questions for Les Bleus' number 20. And, as a good communicator, Kylian did not hold back. He was in seventh heaven, but he did not let it show too much. He did not allow himself to get caught up in the euphoria of the moment and kept his tone measured. Always with a pasted-on smile. Only once did he make a funny face in front of the microphones, a grimace, but he quickly caught himself. It was when they asked him: 'Are you fully committed to football now?'

'I've always been fully committed to my football. You're the ones who thought my head was somewhere else. Football is where I express myself best. It's the only thing I can do and it's what I enjoy most. It's been so great to get back on the pitch again. Sitting on the bench was making my feet itch.'

Kylian had not had the pleasure of taking to the turf since those 74 minutes against Toulouse. On 13 August against Dijon, the second game of the league season, he had spent the whole 90 minutes on the bench. Leonardo Jardim had picked Adama Diakhaby instead. In the press conference, the Portuguese manager explained his choice: 'It was a decision made by the club not to let him play. When I talk about the club, I mean the whole club, the decision-makers.' In short, the order not to play the boy had come from the upper echelons: President Rybolovlev and Vice President Vasilyev.

Why would they make such a decision? Because the relationship between the Mbappé family and the principality club's directors was by then extremely tense. The fact that Kylian had chosen Paris Saint-Germain was now in the public domain, or almost. It had been announced by *Paris United* and reported by both *Marca* and *L'Équipe*, who had made it their front page on 11 August. There was a large photo of Kylian with his arms folded, looking up at the Paris club's new number 10, with the headline: 'Mbappé wants to play with Neymar.' The subtitle went into more detail: 'The arrival of the Brazilian, coupled with PSG's Champions League ambitions, were what eventually convinced the Monegasque prodigy he wanted to come to the capital. The prospect of another transfer for around €180 million has not been well received by other European clubs.'

The article went on to claim that the Mbappé family, after waiting in vain to receive a counter-offer from Barcelona, had told the two other clubs still in the running, Real Madrid and Manchester City (Liverpool and Arsenal had long since fallen away), that they had chosen Paris and informed AS Monaco of the player's desire to play in the French capital. Vadim Vasilyev knew he would have to forget the idea of selling him to Florentino Pérez and get ready to deal with PSG.

This was the prospect that pleased the Mediterranean club the least. The idea of strengthening a direct opponent was hard to swallow for the Monegasque directors. They could drag the thing out as much as they liked but, whether they were keen to or not, they would have to negotiate with the Paris club because Wilfrid Mbappé and Antero Henrique, PSG's sporting director, had apparently come to an agreement in principle based on a five-year contract and a gross annual salary of €18 million, the club's second highest after that of Neymar. Just a tad higher than the €700,000 per month said to have been offered by Monaco or the €6 million offered by Real Madrid. Mbappé senior had also been reassured about Financial Fair Play. He was concerned about possible UEFA sanctions (expulsion from European competition, for example) due to an extremely expensive and unprecedented shopping campaign, but Antero Henrique calmed him down by guaranteeing that PSG had the financial means to cope with another multimillion euro deal.

In other words, the Mbappé clan were convinced that Paris was the place for them. But no one in Monaco was either convinced or happy about it. Firstly, they decided to punish the boy who wanted to do his own thing and wasn't prepared to back down. Yet again, Jardim was forced to provide an explanation at a press conference. This time on 16 August, two days before an away game at Metz.

'We've never been in the habit of punishing our players. That's not the right word. It was more about protecting him. With everything going on around this eighteen-year-old kid, it's our responsibility to protect him from the storm around him,' said the Portuguese manager. He then added, for the benefit of the journalists: 'Kylian isn't 100 per cent, he's not fit at the moment and that's to be expected. If another newspaper offered you fifteen times your salary, your fingers wouldn't move around your laptop keyboards quite so smoothly!'

So, in order to protect his number 29 from the media whirlwind around him, Jardim overlooked Kylian for the game against Metz. Some media outlets were also reporting that there had been a training ground bust-up between Kylian and Andrea Raggi, something that was said to have resulted in the striker being sent off. That the kid from Bondy was on edge was not up for discussion. The reason why was soon revealed: he was unable to do what he loved best, play football. His manager criticised him openly to the press, as well as in front of his teammates. To make matters worse, he was no longer the main player in the saga, and, according to his uncle Pierre Mbappé, who knew him very well, he liked to be in control of his own life.

Another bout of misery came on 27 August. Kylian

watched on from the bench as his team took a 6–1 beating at the hands of OM. He didn't spend a single minute on the pitch.

On 28 August, Mbappé, called up to play for France in two World Cup qualifiers, arrived at Clairefontaine. Didier Deschamps was convinced that the boy was in the right frame of mind and that, despite all the transfer rumours, he was focused on playing for Les Bleus. Or so he responded when asked what Kylian was doing in the France team when he hadn't played for almost a month. Obviously, the manager was careful not to provide any information about a possible transfer to PSG. All he said was: 'Kylian Mbappé is currently still a Monaco player,' but he did involuntarily confirm that a deal would be done: 'The future will tell us if he's made the right choice, but it is his choice, as you know. He doesn't feel ready to go abroad and that's up to him based on the analysis he's done. He's coming off six extraordinary months with Monaco and he needs a little bit more time to confirm it. You won't complain that he is staying in France. He's changing clubs but staying in Ligue 1.'

Too bad that not everything had been neither said nor done. Monaco were still in negotiations with PSG and although they had initially accepted the proposal from the Parisian club they later retracted it and vetoed the transfer. So much so that overnight between 30 and 31 August, there was still no talk of an agreement. These were the last crazy hours of the transfer window. Also competing for the boy from Bondy were Barcelona, who had bagged Ousmane Dembélé but had yet failed to seal the deal for Philippe Coutinho. According to *L'Équipe*, a private jet was on stand-by on the tarmac at Paris's Le Bourget airport waiting to take the Mbappé family to Ciudad Condal to sign a possible agreement. But in the end the plane never took off.

At 6.30pm on 31 August 2017, a photo of Kylian appeared on the principality club's website with a two-line caption: 'AS Monaco wish all the best for the future to @KMbappe who is joining @PSG_inside! #MerciKylian.'

A minute later it was the turn of the club in the capital: 'Paris Saint-Germain are delighted to announce the signing of Kylian Mbappé! #BienvenueKylian.'

After four years, almost two seasons as a professional, 58 games, 27 goals and sixteen assists, the little gem of French football was saying goodbye to the principality. He arrived in Paris on the basis of a season-long loan with a subsequent purchase option of €180 million. A formula that allowed PSG to circumvent the risk of contravening Financial Fair Play regulations after the €222 million paid for Neymar. The €180 million would go into the summer 2018 account books. Mbappé would sign a contract tying him to the Parisian club until 30 June 2022. He had become the second most expensive footballer in footballing history, behind

Neymar, and the most expensive transfer between two French clubs.

At 10.17pm on 31 August 2017, Kylian Mbappé came on in place of Olivier Giroud. It was the 75th minute of the game and France were 2–0 up against Holland, thanks to goals from Antoine Griezmann and Thomas Lemar. Barely two minutes later and PSG's newest player almost scored with his first touch following a move by Layvin Kurzawa. He had been let off the leash and was very keen to play, that much was clear. Every time he slalomed off, he sowed panic in the defence of his opposition, reduced to ten men after the sending off of Kevin Strootman for a foul on Griezmann.

At 10.32pm, in the 91st minute of the game, with the score at 3–0 thanks to another goal from Lemar, the boy from Bondy scored his first goal in a blue shirt. His devastating pace down the right wing had baffled the orange defender who had no idea where to look. A one-two with his former teammate Djibril Sidibé and a shot with the side of his right foot saw him thread the ball past poor Jasper Cillessen. It was only his fifth cap and his seventh shot on goal. He ran to the stands and performed his usual celebration with his hands under his arms. He was the youngest scorer in a France shirt after George Lech, the RC Lens player, who had scored his first international goal against Switzerland on 11 November 1963, aged eighteen years and five months (Kylian was eighteen years and eight months old).

If Thursday 31 August really had been a great day for Mbappé, Sunday 3 September would not be quite so good. In Toulouse, against modest Luxembourg, France racked up 76 per cent of the possession, 34 shots and 635 passes, but the match ended in a lacklustre 0–0 draw. After passing the test against the Dutch, it was a result that no one was expecting. Kylian started on the right wing in Deschamps' 4-4-2 formation. It was not his usual position and he, in fact, ended up drifting to the left and into the centre, stomping on the boots of his teammates. Despite this, he was the most dangerous of Les Bleus' strike force in the first half. In the twelfth minute, he provided Griezmann with a stunning assist that the Atlético Madrid player fired into the stands, then got himself noticed with runs in the eighteenth and 22nd minutes. He remained on the pitch until the 59th minute, when Deschamps decided to substitute him with Kingsley Coman. The verdict on the number 20's performance was good; for many he had been the best, together with Lemar. It was a shame about the result. It was a shame for France that they would have to wait to beat Belarus on 10 October to secure their ticket for Russia 2018.

Three days after the fiasco of the France team in Toulouse, Kylian Mbappé was crowned in Paris. There was a full house, almost as there had been for Neymar, in the auditorium at the Parc des Princes for the official unveiling of PSG's new player. Nasser Al-Khelaifi, the president, did the honours.

'Hello everyone. I'm delighted to be here with you, this is a big day for us. We're very happy to introduce you to Kylian Mbappé, our newest recruit. This is a great moment for the club, for Ligue 1 and for every club in France. He's only eighteen but the whole world already knows him. It was impossible for me to accept that he wouldn't stay in France because Kylian is already a great talent and a great young hope for France.' Al-Khelaifi paused for effect and continued as two photos of Kylian visiting the Parc des Princes as a child appeared on the screen. 'People don't know why Kylian chose Paris, perhaps they will if they look at the two photos up there. He's on familiar ground here because Paris is his city and PSG is the club in his heart. Kylian, welcome home, welcome to Paris, to PSG and to the Parc.'

Next came the turn of the boy worth €180 million.

He was wearing a dark blue suit, white shirt and dark tie, an elegant and formal outfit which echoed that of the president, apart from the fact that the knot of his tie was not quite perfect. With his hands entwined and sitting upright in front of the microphone, the eighteen year old began his monologue:

'Hello everyone. As you know, it's a great pleasure for me to be joining PSG, one of the best clubs in the world. It's an extremely ambitious club. They want to become the very best and aren't content just to want it. They've put all the ingredients in place to try to make it happen and their plans are more than solid. This is what attracted me. It's also important that I'm staying in France after only six months in top-flight football. It was also important to come home, to the city where I was born and where I grew up. With PSG, with lots of hard work, respect and humility, we can achieve our goals of winning lots of trophies and the dream that drives everyone at the club: the Champions League. I'm really happy and I want to thank you all for being here.'

This was followed by thanks to his family, lawyers and everyone at PSG who had helped make his transfer a reality.

Next came the turn of the journalists' questions. The first: 'At the end of last season we had the impression that you wanted to stay in Monaco for one more season. What changed to mean that you're sitting here in front of us today?'

'To be honest with you, when I finished my season in May with the league title, I was pretty sure I was going to stay. When I spoke with the president at the very beginning, I made Monaco my priority. I met with him and told him that staying was my priority. But certain things happened that made me change my position a lot. What happened was simple but this is neither the time nor the place to talk about it. I will do so in due course. I know that lots of people are waiting and have questions, which is understandable because it's been a hot topic all summer, but I'll talk about it very soon and explain everything that happened. I spent a lot of time planning my future with my family and I made the decision to join PSG. I think it's the best choice for me because the club's plans will allow me to develop and to learn while winning. Learning is all very well but you have to win. You only get one career and it goes quickly. I'm hungry to win titles. I'm a competitor who wants to win, year after year and day after day, so I want to learn and continue learning but I want to win, and right now.'

More and more hands went up in the audience as questions came from all sides about Unai Emery, his new manager; about Neymar and how much his arrival at PSG had influenced Kylian's decision; about the boy's ambitions for the new season; about how prepared he was to handle the pressure. There was something for everyone and, of course, there was the small matter of the €180 million.

'That question comes up a lot and I always have the same response,' said Kylian. 'I don't handle everything, it's not my job, so it's not something I deal with. The price is by-the-by as far as I'm concerned. It's not going to change how I live or think, and even less how I play. The money doesn't go into my pocket and it hasn't come out of it either. It's not something I'm going to worry about. I'm just going to go out on the pitch and I think playing with players like that will actually make me feel free and I'll enjoy it more.'

The press conference was coming to an end and the questions became lighter: 'Will your mother be taking you to training here like she did in Monaco?' 'No, the club's given me a driver.'

'Are you going to go back home to live with your parents?' 'I'm staying in a hotel at the moment but we're going to find a house for the whole family. A family house, not just with mum and dad.'

Twenty-one minutes had passed since the start of the press conference; Kylian was talking about the Parc des Princes, where he would often go when he had pocket money to pay for his ticket or when his brother was playing against PSG, when a press officer came onto the stage with a reminder that the president and player were expected on the pitch for the official photo.

At first, Kylian stood next to Nasser Al-Khelaifi, with the PSG number 29 shirt clearly in shot. Next he was on his own, then with Wilfrid and Ethan, and then finally with his father, brother, Uncle Pierre and his little cousin. After the photos, he stepped out onto the red carpet outside the stadium to greet the fans. Wearing an '*Ici, c'est Paris*' scarf, he shook hands, signed autographs, took photos, bowed and even jumped up and down. '*Mbappé allez, allez, allez!*' sang the ultras. Kylian the Communicator played along.

Chapter 15

Donatello

It was all Presnel Kimpembe's fault. He was the one who started it. The defender from Beaumont-sur-Oise was responsible for plenty of the laughs at the back of the team coach. With his dark, cropped hair, a pair of large headphones over his ears and a friendly attitude, it was hard not to like him. After that, everyone else started using the same nickname for Kylian, from Dani Alves to Neymar, even the captain Thiago Silva, who prepared a surprise for the player not long afterwards: a luxury Dior box containing a Donatello mask: one of the four Teenage Mutant Ninja Turtles, from the comic books created by the American publisher Mirage Studios in 1984, that had since spawned a cartoon series and various films. It is worth remembering that Donatello, who wears a purple mask, is particularly skilled at handling a *bō* (a wooden staff used in jiu-jitsu, the Japanese martial art) and is the intellectual of the group that also comprises his brothers Michelangelo, Raphael and Leonardo. But, like them, he loves eating pizza at any time of the day and night.

Kylian's baptism as Donatello happened during the first few days of his new life at PSG. 'We gave him the nickname because he looks a bit like a turtle,' explains Adrien Rabiot. 'It was meant kindly, he took it well,' adds Paris Saint-Germain's number 25. In all honesty, Mbappé did not seem particularly keen on the nickname they had given him, but he did take it well: 'It's a nickname that made me laugh. It's a good sign of friendship and it helps overcome match tension in the dressing room.'

Chants of 'Donatello! Donatello!' accompanied by the percussion of glasses ring out loud and clear on the evening of 7 September, the eve of the league game against Metz and Kylian's debut in a Paris Saint-Germain shirt. The squad is having dinner as images of a handball game play on a big screen on the back wall. But no one seems particularly interested. They are all clamouring for Donatello to give his speech. It is the traditional initiation to which all dressing room newcomers are subjected. Hazing, like military recruits and university freshmen, a vestige of the past and a rite of passage that survives in the world of French football and elsewhere.

Incited by his teammates, the boy from Bondy, wearing a red tracksuit top, stands on a chair at the end of the table, holding a bottle of mineral water, and takes the microphone: 'Let me introduce myself, my name is Kylian. I'm eighteen and I'm a new player.' He then moves on to his song. The new Paris number 29 performs: *C'est plus l'heure* by Mr Franglish, featuring Dadju and Vegeta, the same melody he sang for his initiation with the France team. By now, he's almost a professional! He sings the chorus:

Après l'heure, c'est plus l'heure
J'ai demandé ta main
Tu me l'as pas donnée (oh oh ah)
Grosse erreur
J'aurai pu devenir l'homme qui t'a tout donné

(There's no time but the right time / I asked for your hand, you didn't give it to me (oh oh ah) / Big mistake / I could've been the man to give you everything); he knows it off by heart.

The less said about the performance the better! Who knows what Mr Franglish, a rapper originally from Paris's twentieth *arrondissement*, would have said. The gestures and look on the face of Dani Alves perhaps indicate that his judgement may not have been all that positive, but the newcomer's performance is greeted by applause and drumming on the table all the same. Marco Verratti, the Italian in the group, enjoyed the event and posted the video on Twitter at 9.46pm. By that time the following night, on 8 September 2017, the show Kylian had put on at the Stade Saint-Symphorien would be far more successful. And the best was yet to come.

At 8.05pm, he came out of the dressing room tunnel to whistles from the home fans. Wearing a blue track-suit top and yellow shorts, he was followed by Neymar Junior. Mr €222 million had only landed in France on the Wednesday, after his commitments with the Brazilian national team against Ecuador and Colombia. His presence in the starting eleven had remained uncertain until the last minute, but in the end he was included. Shortly before the game, he posted a selfie with Kylian on the tarmac at the airport. The boy from Bondy, smiling in his headphones, points to his team-mate as Ney makes the famous shaka sign. Everything points to a complicity between the pair. Something that later becomes apparent on the pitch.

With the ball at his feet, PSG's number 29 began warming up with his teammates. He had trained with them very little, barely six days since arriving at the club in the French capital, and given the international com-mitments of Neymar and Cavani, had only coincided with them on the pitch once or twice. Instincts still needed to kick in. It is not hard to imagine the huge pressure, the excitement that this first game with the Parisian team must have represented for the boy worth €180 million. He knew that his performance would be scrutinised under a microscope, analysed minute by minute, move by move, technical detail by technical detail, kilometres run, successful passes, unsuccessful passes, dribbling attempts, shots on target or wide of goal. Everyone, pundits and fans alike, was trying to understand if the eighteen year old really was worth his price tag and if he could stand up to comparison with the number 10 and 'El Matador'. But Kylian is determined and has always been someone who knows what he wants. 'I told myself I would have to make an impression from the very first game. And that's what I did. It was important to get on with the people around me straight away,' he would confess to *France Football* months later.

The fourth league game of the season, between Metz and PSG, kicked off at 8.45pm. Unai Emery had picked a team with a solid gold attack. Edinson Cavani, who had returned from Uruguay the day before, led the way, with Kylian Mbappé on the right and Neymar on the left. It was the debut of a stellar strike force worth €466 million. Not counting the €45 million paid for Julian Draxler, the German, who slotted in just behind the trio.

The Parisians were playing against the team propping up Ligue 1: Metz had still to win a match. The memory of the hat-trick he had scored against Metz in a Monaco shirt the previous season was still fresh in Kylian's mind.

On your marks, go. After three minutes of play, Kylian was dancing along the left touchline, trying to get past two opponents, but the Metz number 25 got the better of him with a foul.

The sixth minute saw a double one-two down the middle on the edge of the area between Neymar and Mbappé, but the final pass was intercepted. In the fourteenth minute, another impressive and extremely fast exchange between the Brazilian and Frenchman came off. It was just the beginning of a long series of close exchanges between the two teammates. None of them would provide concrete results, but the opposing team were struggling to cope. By the time the game was over, Neymar and Mbappé would be voluntarily seeking each other out on a regular basis, with a total of 36 passes between the pair. The most prolific relationship on the pitch. It was a good sign for the future.

The sought-after goal came in the 31st minute. Neymar opened things up for Mbappé and Cavani. They were both on the ball, but the former, as a question of hierarchy, left his colleague the honour and glory of controlling the ball and taking the winning strike. It was the seventh goal since the start of the season for El Matador, who immediately went over to hug the new arrival to thank him for his kindness. In the 33rd minute, the boy offered a wonderful back-heel pass to Edinson, but this time its conclusion was handled easily by Kawashima, the Metz keeper. A minute later and Kylian tried again: he set off on a solo run down the left wing and eventually brushed a perfect cross with the outside of his right foot on to the head of the Uruguayan, who fired the ball with complete freedom. The goal seemed a done deal, but Kawashima flew to a save. In the 35th minute, Neymar put in a cross from the right of the area, but the header from the number 29 left the ball far from Metz's goal. The home team soon equalised: Mathieu Dossevi found a way through on the right to get in a cross for Emmanuel Rivière, on the opposite side, who anticipated Rabiot and beat Alphonse Areola. One–one, an unexpected scenario.

Just before half-time, the pairing of Mbappé and Neymar pulled off another lightening counter-attack. With space to run in the middle of the pitch, Kylian put on a burst of pace, took the ball with him and fed the number 10 on the left. It was a diagonal and well-directed shot, but Kawashima pulled off a fingertip save to deflect it for a corner.

The second half began with a header from Areola that was pure madness. On the end of a back-pass from Marquinhos, the Parisian keeper decided to use his head instead of his foot to serve Kimpembe, inadvertently providing a spectacular assist for Rivière in the middle of the box. But the Metz striker fired the ball over the open goal he had been gifted by his opponents and into the stands. Benoit Assou Ekotto then got himself sent off for a nasty tackle on Mbappé, who had set off on a run down the right wing. The boy from Bondy was rolling around on the grass but then managed to continue without difficulty, while the Cameroon defender left the pitch. Metz found themselves down to ten men and without a manager as Philippe Hinschberger was also sent off. The momentum of the match changed. PSG took control of the ball and Kylian went on to score. In the 59th minute, the new Parisian tried to pick out Neymar in the area with a lob. The ball came back off a defender to Kylian who tried a crisp, low volley with his right foot. It was 2–1 and the striker's story with his new team had begun. With his hands under his arms in front of the fans, the little gem of French football celebrated his first goal in a yellow shirt. Cavani jumped on his back, Neymar hugged him and Kylian lifted him up.

But it wasn't over yet: in the 61st minute, his second goal seemed like a sure thing. On his own in the area, Neymar stopped, waited for the number 29 to arrive and teed it up for him. The boy unleashed a powerful shot. Kawashima was beaten but Niakhate, who was out of position, turned his back as the ball hit him and flew out. Neymar stepped up, received the ball from Rabiot and tried a right-footed shot from the edge of the area. It was unstoppable. There was still time and Kylian involuntarily provided the perfect assist for Cavani's second goal. The cross came in from the left, rebounded between a defender's leg and Mbappé's arm as the Uruguayan, who had been following the move, managed to toe-poke the ball into the net. Lucas Moura closed PSG's account in the 87th minute. Five–one,

PSG's fifth victory of the league season and a perfect debut for the new arrival, who talked about his performance for the Canal+ microphones.

'It was a great first goal. I was trying to pass to Ney but the defender got in the way. I reacted more quickly than my opponent and fired it in. I always said I wanted to play with great players. Now I'm playing with the best in the league and maybe in Europe. I'm learning from how they move and their professionalism to do my best on the pitch. All I wanted was to be on the pitch and the manager made that decision. I really enjoyed it today. I'm delighted, really happy with how I did.'

His new teammates were happy too. Take Kimpembe, for example, and his Instagram post: 'Congratulations on your first goal! Donatello strikes again and pizza will be your reward.'

Chapter 16

MCN

There were three questions that came up immediately. The first was the most futile but also the most fun: what would the three-pronged attack be called? How could you begin to describe this trio of wonders? What was the right name for PSG's new strike force? Was there a suitable nickname for Neymar, Cavani and Mbappé? How could such an explosive attack be summed up?

From the moment Kylian had arrived at PSG there had been plenty of discussion on the subject, both seriously and not so, starting at *L'Équipe*. All sorts of things were suggested. MCN was the easy solution, in keeping with the recent strike forces of Real Madrid's BBC (Bale, Benzema and Cristiano Ronaldo) and Barcelona's MSN (Messi, Suárez and Neymar). But MCN was not particularly memorable, unlike BBC (thanks to its handy similarity to the British Broadcasting Corporation) or MSN (Microsoft's web portal).

MCN stands for either Maritime Campus Netherlands or Montage Cable Network, an African TV channel. In other words, nothing particularly glamorous. Then came another solution: KEN. Apart from the fact that it used two first names and one surname, it immediately made people think of Ken, the Mattel doll and Barbie's eternal boyfriend. These were simple acronyms, but perhaps it was better not to put limits on imagination. As Mbappé had been given the nickname Donatello, some suggested naming all three after the Ninja Turtles. But there are four Ninja Turtles and, apart from Kylian, the others did not look much like Michelangelo, Raphael or Leonardo. Because of the French connection, someone had the bright idea of dusting off Alexandre Dumas' three musketeers. But how would that work with D'Artagnan? And besides, the nickname had already been used in French sport for the Four Musketeers (Jean Borotra, Jacques Brugnon, Henri Cochet and René Lacoste), the tennis players who won the Davis Cup six times in a row between 1927 and 1932. Suggestions from the serious to the facetious appeared from all sides: the infernal trio, the knights of the apocalypse, the three tenors, 9-10-29, the trident of dreams or the Holy Trinity, to name but a few. But eventually, MCN was chosen, either that or simply Mbappé-Cavani-Neymar, with a hyphen between their names.

Now for the second question. And this one was serious. Could the so-called MCN be the best attack in football? After only six games in which the trio had played together, the answer could only be a yes.

The details of how things had gone in both Ligue 1 and the Champions League were as follows ... Against

Metz (5–1), their first outing together, they had scored three goals (two from Cavani and one from Mbappé). On 12 September at Glasgow's Celtic Park, the start of the Champions League group stage, the three players put on a spectacular display. The Scottish team fell to their heaviest ever home defeat in a European game, conceding five goals. Neymar got things started, followed by Kylian, who scored his second goal for PSG on the end of a header from the number 10. Cavani took care of making things worse from the penalty spot, then followed that with a header towards the end of the game. Mikael Lustig also lent a hand, giving PSG their fourth with an own goal. The MCN had scored six goals in just two games.

In the league, against Olympique Lyonnais, their first heavyweight opponents, none of the three scored on 17 September. But PSG won 2–0 thanks to Marcelo and Jérémy Morel. Both were own goals, the first instigated by Cavani (Marcelo deflected it into his own goal); the second from a shot by Mbappé that rebounded between Anthony Lopes's foot and Morel's leg to end up in the back of the net. For the record, El Matador hit the crossbar with a penalty awarded for a foul on Kylian. On 23 September, Neymar missed the game in Montpellier through injury. It ended 0–0. After six consecutive victories, it was the Parisian's first draw but it would be remedied four days later on Wednesday 27 September at the Parc des Princes.

This time their opponents were one of the greats of the old continent. The Bayern Munich of Thomas Müller, Robert Lewandowski and James Rodríguez. With another Champions League veteran on the bench: Carlo Ancelotti. For PSG's front trio it was a trial by fire, the perfect test to see how good they could be. After only two minutes, the Bavarians were already behind, thanks to Neymar: he forged into the area from the left, attracting a swarm of opponents who stuck to him, leaving Dani Alves completely unmarked on the right; served to perfection by the number 10, he slotted the ball between the legs of Ulreich. In the 31st minute, Mbappé ran down the left wing and into the box with two opponents on his shoulder, but turned and, with a subtle touch, served the rapidly arriving Cavani, who found the winning shot. The job was completed by the pairing of Kylian and Neymar. The number 29 did all the hard work on his own: he slipped between two Bavarians and, as the keeper came out, slotted the ball diagonally into the centre. The defenders were like statues as Neymar beat them to it to score.

The MCN were starting to strike fear into European hearts. Not to mention French hearts, as was clear from how the club from the capital battered the Girondins de Bordeaux, the third-placed team in Ligue 1 and unbeaten at that time. On 30 September, the Girondins may have scored twice but they let in six. The celebration began with a sweet free-kick that kissed the crossbar and blew the cobwebs off the corner of the goalposts. Again, Neymar was responsible. In the twelfth minute, an Mbappé back-heel to the Brazilian played in El Matador to make it 2–0. The third came from Thomas Meunier. The Girondins came to life and scored to make it 3–1, but Neymar gave PSG back their cushion from the penalty spot. Then came a goal from Julian Draxler. After just 45 minutes, the score was 5–1: it was the first time PSG had scored so many in a first half. The sixth came from Kylian, who dedicated it to Benjamin Mendy, his former Monaco teammate who had suffered a nasty injury a few days earlier against Crystal Palace (rupturing the cruciate ligaments in his knee). He would be out for almost the entire season. The boy from Bondy had scored his second league goal in a PSG shirt and reminded everyone of that fact by holding up two fingers as he thought of his unfortunate friend.

At this point in the story there is something to be gained from taking stock and reviewing statistics to discover that, with fourteen goals and six assists, the MCN were ahead of even the most famous attacking trio of recent times: the MSN. Messi, Suárez and Neymar, in the 2014–15 season, their first together, had sent records tumbling when, after only six games – four in the Liga and two in the Champions League (Ajax and Hapoel) – they had racked up twelve goals and six assists between them.

For Mbappé, Cavani and Neymar the winning streak continued. Away from home, on 14 October, against Dijon, PSG won 2–1, despite some difficulty, thanks to two goals from Thomas Meunier. Cavani was not on the pitch, Neymar failed to shine and this time Mbappé saw himself denied twice by Reynet, the opposing keeper. The three superstars were back in action in the Champions League against the Belgian team Anderlecht. After only 160 seconds of play, Verratti provided Kylian with an assist for a razor sharp shot: eight goals in twelve Champions League appearances. Not bad for a kid! Similar things had been achieved by the likes of Karim Benzema, Radamel Falcao and Cavani himself. As half-time approached, the three tenors were conducting the orchestra: a Neymar rocket came in from the edge of the area but was somehow parried by Sels onto the head of Mbappé, who set up Cavani to make it 2–0. Then came the number 10, who sent a low free-kick under the wall to make it three. Ángel Di María then added to the MCN show.

PSG had yet to drop a point in the Champions League and were dominating domestically. The trio were scoring an avalanche of goals and a third question began doing the rounds: would they succeed in becoming one of the greatest attacking trios in footballing history? By way of preparation, what follows is a brief look at their competition. Everyone has their individual preferences and tastes, depending on latitude and longitude, where you live, who you support, your favourite colours, how many seasons you have seen go by, your favourite style of play or the things you love and hate. But some trios, whether you agree or not, are milestones in the history of the round ball.

Thinking back to football in black and white, how could we forget the 'Aranycsapat', the Golden Team, the Hungarian national team of the 1950s? With its three forwards; Ferenc Puskás, Sándor Kocsis and Nándor Hidegkuti? Players who, at Wembley in 1953, defeated the inventors of football 6–3 and, in 1954, lost somewhat inexplicably in the World Cup final against Germany.

The late 1950s saw the emergence of Didi, Vavá and Pelé, the Brazilians who amazed the world in 1958 and 1962. Edson Arantes do Nascimiento with his dribbling and goal scoring, Didi running down the wing and Vavá as a pure centre forward. And let's not forget a certain Garrincha, who had tricks of all sorts up his sleeve. During the same period, this time in Spain, Madrid to be precise, a fairy-tale trio was formed in 1958: Alfredo di Stéfano, the Argentine, known as 'The Blond Arrow', Ferenc Puskás, the Hungarian, known as 'The Galloping Major' and Paco Gento, the Spaniard, on the left wing. Wearing Real Madrid shirts, they would win a fifth consecutive European Cup for Los Blancos against Eintracht Frankfurt.

In England, in the mid-1960s, came the Holy Trinity

of the Red Devils: George Best, the flawed Northern Irish genius, Bobby Charlton, one of the greatest goal scorers in Manchester United history, and Denis Law, the finisher. Three men who would win one Ballon d'Or each. Their consecration came in the 1968 European Cup final when they swept away Eusebio's Benfica 4–1. Best, Charlton and Law: a statue of the trio stands in front of Old Trafford. Every United fan has their photo taken under the monument.

In the 1970s, it was the turn of Ajax's total football and the Clockwork Orange. Take Johan Cruyff, the number 14, the aesthete and philosopher of the ball, Johnny Rep on the right wing and Piet Keizer on the left to complete Ajax's 4-3-3 formation. It is hard to forget when, on 30 May 1973, Rep scored in the final at Juventus to give the Amsterdam club its third consecutive European Cup. It is also worth remembering that in 1974, that particular trio took Holland to the World Cup final in what was then West Germany.

Staying with Germany, next came the trio formed by Uli Hoeness, Gerd Müller and Karl-Heinz Rummenigge at Bayern Munich in the mid-1970s. The two blonds and the brown-haired Müller began taking defences apart in 1976, admirably supported by 'Der Kaiser', Franz Beckenbauer. Müller and Rummenigge would both win the Ballon d'Or, the former in 1970 and the latter in 1980 and 1981.

Back to Brazil, because the Brazilians are always in

contention: both in the 1970 World Cup in Mexico – when the Canarinho beat Italy 4–1 in the final with their winning trio of Jairzinho, Tostão and Pelé – and in the 2002 World Cup in Japan and South Korea, when the three Rs of Ronaldinho, Rivaldo and Ronaldo had their day. Ronaldo, 'The Phenomenon', would win the Golden Boot with eight goals, while Rivaldo scored four and Ronaldinho, then at PSG, scored two. David Seaman, the England goalkeeper, would never forget Ronaldinho's spectacular free-kick.

In 2003–4, Arsène Wenger's Gunners won the Premier League without losing a single game. They equalled the record set in the 1888–9 season by Preston North End and were nicknamed 'The Invincibles', thanks to a trio formed by Robert Pires, Dennis Bergkamp and Thierry Henry, who, with 30 league goals, would finish as top scorer.

And now for the recent MSN. In their first season together, Messi, Suárez and Neymar scored 122 goals and took home the Liga, Champions League and Copa del Rey treble. In the three years before Neymar left, they scored 344 goals in 135 matches.

And finally, the BBC, the three who, in the last three seasons, had averaged 100 goals and won the Champions League for two successive years.

Will Mbappé, the little French jewel, Neymar, O Rei 2.0, and Cavani, El Matador, carve out a place for themselves in footballing history? Who knows?

Chapter 17

The Golden Boy

It was 6.50pm on Monday 24 October 2017 when Kylian Mbappé, wearing a black tuxedo, white shirt and bow tie, climbed out of a Mercedes van and went into the Sporting Club in Monte Carlo. He was accompanied by Wilfrid, Fayza and Ethan. The boy from Bondy was back, for one evening, in the city that saw him make his Ligue 1 debut and where he was crowned champion of France. He was going back to his roots to collect the 2017 Golden Boy award. Mbappé had won the trophy that *Tuttosport*, the Turin-based sports daily, had been bestowing on the best Under 21 player in Europe since 2003.

The PSG rookie had blown away the competition with 291 points, almost double those of the player in second place, his compatriot Ousmane Dembélé, recently purchased by Barcelona, who had received 149. In third place was Marcus Rashford, the Manchester United star, with 76 points. Just off the podium, in fourth place, came Gabriel Jesus, Manchester City's São Paulo-born player (72 points). It was an apotheosis for

PSG's number 29: out of 35 voters, only three had failed to rank him first. It was a landslide the likes of which had never been seen before. Mbappé was following in the footsteps of the 2016 winner Renato Sanches, the Portuguese midfielder on loan from Bayern Munich to Swansea City. He was joining a golden roll of honour that included, among others, the names of Wayne Rooney (2004), Lionel Messi (2005), Cesc Fàbregas (2006), Mario Götze (2011), Isco (2012), Paul Pogba (2013) and Anthony Martial (2015).

But before this 'star-studded night', the Paris striker had come in for his first heavy bout of criticism from the French press. Contrary winds had been blowing forcefully since the away game at Dijon on 14 October. 'For the first time since exploding in Ligue 1, Kylian disappointed us.' 'Invisible for the first 45 minutes, he made a startling number of mistakes in the second half.' 'Of course, having to spearhead the Paris attack due to the absence of Edinson Cavani did not go in his favour, but he made some uncharacteristic mistakes in front of goal.' The media and pundits did not hold back.

Unai Emery, his manager, came to his defence: 'You think Mbappé isn't playing as well at the moment? No. Mbappé is a young player who will make progress as he gains more experience. It will be very positive for him. He missed a lot of chances against Dijon, but that's part of the experience, part of his journey. He's smart and everyone likes him. He brings something to the team in terms of assists and combinations, as well as in front of goal.' On the eve of the Champions League game against Anderlecht, the Spanish manager then added: 'If he has the same scoring chances tomorrow, he'll definitely be able to convert them.'

He was right to have faith. Away to the Belgians, in the third minute, after a fine piece of combination play with Marco Verratti, Kylian broke the deadlock and opened the way to a convincing 4–0 win. PSG had hit their stride in Group B, but the goal failed to bring an end to the controversy. The worst was yet to come.

And come it did in the evening of Sunday 22 October against OM at the Vélodrome. 'Mbappé played his worst match since joining PSG'; 'Without a doubt, his worst performance for a year'; 'One of the worst games of his young career'; 'He really, really failed to shine'; 'Missed chances in front of goal, put in no defensive work and had a certain nonchalance on the ball. His first "Clásico" passed Kylian by.' *L'Équipe* awarded him a score of two out of ten.

It was not only his performance on the pitch that attracted the wrath of the press, there was also the fact that the new PSG player, always seemingly aware of how to communicate, showed a different side to himself during a row. After the final whistle, Kylian, cautioned for having taken the referee by the arm to demand a penalty, accused the man in black of being 'substandard'.

The scathing judgements rained down. There was talk of arrogance, self-importance and a boy who, in the space of just a few weeks, had gone from a 'young man doing well in all respects to a big-headed adolescent'. There were insinuations that Neymar was a bad influence, that the Brazilian had even 'contaminated his brain' and that Kylian now saw himself as a Neymar 3.0. In short, the word was that fame had gone to his head and that Kylian was not necessarily the 'French star' everyone thought he was. This is the kind of thing that happens when a footballer who has caused a sensation fails to score for two league games and is not playing at his usual level.

By all appearances, Kylian did not seem unduly concerned. In fact, he even seemed able to turn the tables. He thought about it and came to the conclusion that more than 90 per cent of players go two games or more without scoring, but no one criticises them, so if he was being put under so much pressure, it must be a good thing. It was a sign that his level had gone up and his status had changed; he was now an important player of whom much was expected.

So there he was, smiling, wearing a white Nike t-shirt printed with the number 97005, waiting to receive the entire *Tuttosport* delegation in his Monaco hotel room before the awards ceremony. As his mother Fayza closed the bedroom door while a curious Ethan kept trying to peek, Kylian was given a plaque of *Tuttosport*'s history-making front page and said thank you, with a laugh, in more than passable Italian.

Photos, handshakes, autographs and an exclusive interview for the Turin newspaper followed. Le Petit Prince talked about all sorts of things. About Monaco, PSG, the France national team, the Champions League, Italian football, previous winners of the Golden Boy and even the recent criticism he had come in for. 'I understand very well,' he said, 'that people expect a lot from me in every game, but it's hard for a player to be at their highest level in every match, only the greats manage it. Up to now I've done some great things and if I continue to put in the effort I can do even better. I'm living a dream and I have to take advantage of it and work hard.' He also talked about precocity and his childhood idol: 'Cristiano Ronaldo? Of course, it seems strange that a champion like him never won this prestigious award, but there are some players who mature early on, like Fabregas and Messi, and others who reach their potential later.'

Onto another subject, another example: Thierry Henry. 'I'm honoured by the comparison, but I don't want to be the new Thierry Henry, or the new anyone. I just want to be myself, Kylian Mbappé, and write my own story. Being a copy of someone else is pointless, I want to be an original.' He also talked about his relationship with Neymar. 'It's an honour that Neymar holds me so highly. He knows I admire and love him.

And when a player like him takes you under their wing, you have all the credentials you need to progress. I think he had a fantastic experience in Barcelona, where he won everything. And I want to win everything with Paris Saint-Germain, so, for me, learning from Neymar is the best way to make progress and achieve my goals.'

And so, here was the ambitious eighteen year old in the Salle des Étoiles at Monaco's Sporting club. When his name was called, he left his table and climbed onto the stage where people such as Frank Sinatra, Charles Aznavour, Stevie Wonder, Elton John and Joe Cocker have all performed, to collect the European Golden Boy 2017 award. Emotional, in front of an audience of 300 invited guests, including Leonardo Jardim, his former manager, and Vadim Vasilyev, Vice President of AS Monaco, he received the trophy, a heavy golden ball, from Paolo De Paola, Director of *Tuttosport*. It was 8.25pm.

'I would like to dedicate this to my little brother Ethan, who is in the audience,' said Kylian, who could see another gift arriving, a signed Cristiano Ronaldo shirt. Wilfrid, Kylian's father, told the microphones: 'We are very happy. Today is the reward for his talent and all the hard work put in by our family. No, I'm not surprised by Kylian, the only surprise is that it's all happened so quickly. But the things he's doing now he used to do when he was a child, as those who saw him play back then well know.'

'It really is an honour to have won this award and being in Monaco is almost symbolic. It's one more motivation to keep working hard,' explained Kylian. Then he looked at the trophy in his hands and added: 'I'll put it somewhere on display at home, we've just moved.' One more question: 'Will you win the Ballon d'Or next?' 'I don't know, I can't see into the future,' dodged the boy from Bondy.

But the future was just around the corner.

France Football unveiled the Ballon d'Or classification on 7 December 2017. Cristiano Ronaldo, as had already been revealed, had won his fifth title with 946 points. He had drawn level with Lionel Messi in terms of wins and loudly told the world he was 'the best player in history'. Everyone is free to offer their own opinion on that particular subject; it is for posterity to judge.

The Argentine player, Barcelona's number 10, came second. Neymar, Paris's new star, completed the podium. So far, so predictable; the surprise came with a glance at the top ten. Fourth was Gianluigi Buffon, Juventus's seemingly immortal goalkeeper; fifth, Luka Modrić, the Croat at Real Madrid; sixth, Sergio Ramos the Merengues' captain' and seventh, with 48 points, Kylian Mbappé! PSG's number 29 was ahead of people like Robert Lewandowski, Bayern Munich's Polish striker; Harry Kane, the England centre forward; Edinson Cavani and Luis Suárez, the Uruguayan *matadores*; his national teammates Antoine Griezmann,

N'Golo Kanté and Karim Benzema, and his former Monaco teammate Radamel Falcao.

In addition to the champions he had left in his wake with his incredible half season as a professional, Kylian had beaten yet another age record. By just six days, he was ahead of Michael Owen, the youngest player to be named in the recent history of the award.

With the exception of the Liverpool striker, who finished fourth with his first nomination in 1998, the Parisian prodigy proved to have a clear advantage over most top players, past and present. Take Cristiano Ronaldo, who entered the rankings for the first time in 2004, aged nineteen, and had to be content with twelfth position. Messi was first nominated in 2006, also aged nineteen, in twentieth position. Neymar first appeared in 2011, again aged nineteen, in tenth position. Ronaldo, 'The Phenomenon', eventual winner of two Ballon d'Ors, made his first appearance in the rankings in 1995, aged nineteen, but at no higher than 26th position.

Who would have bet on such a result just a few months earlier? Not even Kylian. When the nominations were announced, the boy drew up his own list and ranked himself between eighteenth and 30th. 'I really never expected seventh. To finish in the top ten with my first nomination is extraordinary. I'm really starting to enter the big league. I have a lot of respect for all those great players, who I was still watching on TV or playing with on my console not so long ago. It's weird …,' Kylian confessed to *France Football*. It was strange, that much was true, so much so that the boy admitted to feeling a bit like a child in front of so many champions, but he did not feel like an intruder. Of course, as his father said, everything had happened at lightning speed; perhaps it had been too fast, but Kylian was not the type to be frightened by what was happening to him.

He turned nineteen on 20 December 2017. He decided to change colour for the occasion and went to 235th Barber Street, a hairdressers and barbers in Boulogne-Billancourt that takes care of the haircuts of Alphonse Areola and Julian Draxler (PSG), Kwadwo Asamoah, Douglas Costa and Blaise Matuidi (Juventus) and Tiémoué Bakayoko (Chelsea). Kylian had his hair dyed blond. A new look – after dallying with something similar last summer – that appeared in pride of place on the barber's Instagram account. He posed with his arms crossed and his hands under his arms in his classic goal celebration. Wearing a red Nike cap and a PSG tracksuit, he entertained his teammates every time he showed off his white hair at the Camps des Loges. With laughs provided by Neymar, jokes, gags and a chorus of '*Bon Anniversaire*' as Kylian blew out the candles of his mini strawberry cake. His birthday was celebrated that same evening at the Parc des Princes. It was the nineteenth game of the season and he was turning nineteen, a perfect coincidence and an excuse to put on a show.

In the 21st minute, he got past two defenders and put his foot down with lightning speed on the right wing to overtake Da Silva before looking up, seeing Cavani in the area and sending him a cross. The Uruguayan finished with a back-heel worthy of Madjer. Stunning! One–nil PSG.

In the 57th minute, Neymar, sporting a plaster on his face, picked up the ball on the left for a pass to Lo Celso, who had sneaked into the area and just about managed to keep the ball from going out for a goal kick before making his cross. With a left-footed volley, Mbappé showed no mercy to Rémy Vercoutre, the Caen keeper.

The game, the last of the year, finished 3–1 to the Parisians. Kylian was man of the match. It brought an end to an impressive December: four goals and three assists in five games. He was celebrating a crazy 2017: 33 goals for club and country across all competitions (twenty with Monaco, twelve with PSG and one with Les Bleus). He was the top French scorer of the year, ahead of Alexandre Lacazette (OL and Arsenal), with 32 goals, and Antoine Griezmann (Atlético Madrid) with 29. Mbappé had scored ten goals in the Champions League and was the youngest footballer to have ever achieved such a feat. He had every right to be happy as he boarded the plane to Doha for PSG's winter training camp. The year 2017 had been his, as even a study carried out by Pressedd showed. Kylian Mbappé was the

French sportsperson who had received the most mentions in the media during 2017. His name had come up an astonishing 44,056 times. He was in first place ahead of Didier Deschamps, Rudi Garcia and Zinedine Zidane. These statistics were even more astonishing when it became clear that in 2016 the boy from Bondy had been in 219th position.

Chapter 18

A treble to wipe Ronaldo
from his memory

PSG had no time to lose. To prepare for what was yet to come, Kylian and his teammates flew to Qatar after the last official match of the year against Caen. The club from the French capital was in Doha for a short three-day training camp in late December. After a promising first half of the season, the club's directors decided to do everything possible to leave their mark on planet football in 2018.

This express trip to the Middle East was first and foremost a communications campaign cleverly orchestrated by their sponsors. The players were transformed into luxury travelling salesmen and appeared all over the city for various marketing opportunities. The most spectacular saw the MCN join captain Thiago Silva for an unlikely game of football tennis played in the middle of the Persian Gulf on a floating platform masquerading as a football pitch. It was a magnificent setting that brought the four stars together in Doha Bay, with its imposing buildings as the backdrop. Kylian was at ease – he posted pictures on social media dressed as an emir – and showed, once again, how easy he found it to adapt. In Qatar, he seemed to return to how he had been when he had first arrived in Monaco, laughing and carefree, in a video that demonstrated how well he got on with Neymar as they travelled to the training ground in a golf buggy. The kid from Bondy also showed his professionalism when it came to discussing his first six months in the French capital in front of TV cameras from all over the world.

How did he feel about the MCN? 'Cavani is the best striker in the world and Neymar is about to become the best player on the planet. How can I not learn and get better by being around them?'

What about life in Paris? 'I can't go out any more. I have to stay at home. Yes, things have changed. It's like I've become a real "star"!' What about the Champions League? 'We know what we're worth, but most importantly we know what we have to do to win a competition like that. There are more and more teams that can win it and we're one of them.'

But he said nothing during the press conference about the upcoming clash with the Real Madrid of his childhood hero, Cristiano Ronaldo. Since the draw for the last sixteen of the Champions League had been made at UEFA headquarters in Switzerland on 11 December, the duel had really captured the imagination of the public, who saw it as a potential transfer of power between the two players. But Kylian had wanted to avoid the two-time defending champions at all costs and would have preferred to face the Swiss team FC Basel at that stage. From the moment he saw the name of the Spanish club appear on his television screen, he could not hide his disappointment. He let out an: 'It's not possible!' before quickly recovering in front of the camera that was following him for a French TV documentary and claiming: 'Let's go! We're up for the fight!'

During his brief stay in Doha, Kylian nevertheless agreed to talk about the two-leg clash between the two heavyweights of European football in an interview with *Marca*. Spain's most popular sports daily put him on its front page on 27 December with the eye-catching headline: 'We're going to Madrid to send a message to the world.' The French international made his ambitions clear throughout the interview:

'We're two of the best teams in the world. They've won the Champions League two years in a row and we're growing [...]. It's a match that could leave its mark on the history of our club against the champions and we're all very motivated. Ronaldo? He was my idol when I was a kid and it was great to meet him when I visited Valdebebas. But I'm a competitor and a competitive person wants to win and keep on winning. It doesn't matter who the opponent is, we just want to win. I loved him when I was little, but that's over now. Now I'm going to the Bernabeu to play and win.'

The groundwork had been laid for the last sixteen game and the growing appetite of France's number one club and its young striker had been confirmed: 'PSG pulled off a veritable *tour de force* in the space of just a few days, with their trip to Qatar and Mbappé's interview in Spain,' said an insider from the Paris club. 'They brought all their financial power and communications ability to bear. Most importantly, they confirmed that their new sporting ambitions are in line with the very aggressive words of their young recruit. It's worth remembering that at that point, Real Madrid were struggling in the Liga and Zinedine Zidane was coming in for plenty of criticism. Many in France thought it was the ideal draw for PSG but that would prove to be a red herring.'

All the more so because, in the run-up to the first leg of this last sixteen game at the Santiago Bernabeu in Madrid, Kylian was far from his best form: while he had started the year at full throttle with two goals and two assists at Rennes as his team began their Coupe de France campaign (1–6), he had since gone under the radar, scoring only one goal against Dijon in the league on 17 January. The former Monaco player had in fact played very little but instead accumulated some hard knocks: first, he had picked up a head injury on 21 January during a violent clash with the Olympique

Lyonnais goalkeeper, Anthony Lopes, then he notched up the first red card of his professional career on 30 January in Rennes in the semi-finals of the League Cup, after the left-winger Ismaïla Sarr had brought him down with an ugly foul that saw him go in on Kylian's calf with his studs.

'It's always better to be playing, that's for sure, but I don't think it's a problem. I'm in the rhythm and I'll be fresh,' said Kylian reassuringly, a few days before the away leg at the Bernabeu. He was in the starting eleven against Real Madrid on 14 February. His game got off to a timid start to say the least, but in the 33rd minute, he was responsible for breaking the deadlock: his pass from the right wing was dealt with poorly by Nacho and Adrien Rabiot surged forward to punish Keylor Navas. Nil–one.

With this fine piece of inspiration, Kylian had unwittingly given the green light to his duel with Cristiano Ronaldo. It was enough to needle the Portuguese player. The five-time Ballon d'Or-winner brought the score line back to 1–1 in the dying moments of the first half by converting a penalty with a powerful strike. When play resumed, it was the Frenchman's turn to shine: Neymar's service was impeccable but Kylian's shot lacked accuracy and Navas parried it as best he could. Missed! It had been a good chance and one that would turn out to be decisive because, at the end of the game, Ronaldo scored a second with his knee before Marcelo made things 3–1. The disappointment was huge for the PSG number 29, especially as, right at the end of the game, he could have made it 3–2 and thrown the last sixteen tie back in the balance, but Real's Costa Rican goalkeeper came out on top for a second time.

Kylian did not need to wait for the verdict from the media to know that the match had passed him by. *L'Équipe* gave him a score of four out of ten, accompanied by the comment: 'He should have been much more effective. He had chances to hurt them. But either because he rushed it or couldn't quite get it right, he was unable to convert.'

The young Parisian striker only had one thing on his mind: getting his revenge two weeks later at the Parc des Princes and joining his illustrious elders Rai, Valdo and Ginola, who had pulled back two late goals against the Madrid team in 1993 to win 4–1 in the return leg of the UEFA Cup quarter-final. Unfortunately, preparation for the second leg was marred by yet more setbacks: on 25 February, Neymar succumbed to a serious injury in a league game and was ruled out for the rest of the season. Three days later, it was Kylian's turn to limp off in the 46th minute against Olympique de Marseille. Suffering from an ankle injury, he was a doubt for a long time: 'The club wanted me to play,' Kylian would later claim in a Canal+ documentary, 'but my family and I talked about it as I didn't want to take any risks.

In the end, after thinking about it a lot, we decided I would play.'

Although Kylian was not at 100 per cent, the decision came close to paying off. On 6 March, at a white hot Parc de Princes, Kylian had a chance to change the game in the 43rd minute. With the score still at 0–0, he picked up a perfect ball on his right in the area as the Madrid defence gave him an unexpected moment of respite. He glanced up and saw Cavani in an ideal position to receive the ball at the near post, but Kylian chose a different option: he tried his luck with a sudden diagonal shot but, as had happened in the first leg, Navas turned it away. The kid from Bondy could only hold his head in his hands as his Uruguayan teammate expressed his dissatisfaction. Although everything had happened very quickly, Kylian's choice had clearly not been the right one. 'In two games he has missed three match-winning chances and shown the gap that still separates him from Cristiano Ronaldo. The Portuguese star eventually opened the scoring at the start of the second half and put an end to the suspense with his third goal against PSG. The two legs had been a complete success for him while Kylian has shown himself to be too weak in his finishing.'

After another 2–1 defeat and a brutal elimination from the Champions League that would cost the club dearly (almost €13 million), this analysis provided by a former PSG player turned out to be kinder than some of the harsh and scoffing comments in certain sections of the media.

Eurosport: 'He didn't live up to expectations. Compared to his idol, Ronaldo, he could see what he still needs to do to be considered a class above.'

So Foot: 'Tonight he looked more like Franklin the Turtle than Donatello. He knows his two times table and how to tie his shoes but there's no one left to supply Cavani.'

'The trial they subjected Kylian to was unfair,' said Lassana Diarra – a former Real midfielder who had joined PSG during the winter transfer window – at the end of the season. 'Of all of us up front, he was the one who was most generous with his teammates. Whenever he could help someone score, he would always provide the right pass. Plus, if he didn't have that team mindset, he could have scored ten more goals this year.'

During the last three months of competition in a PSG shirt, Kylian would bag three more goals in the French league – one against Metz and two against Angers – score twice in the semi-final of the Coupe de France against Caen (1–3) and provide two assists in the League Cup final against AS Monaco in Bordeaux. On 31 March, against his former club, Kylian blocked out the whistles and jeers of the supporters in red and white to serve Di María and Cavani in the convincing 3–0 win.

Failing to catch fire individually at the end of the season, Kylian played for the team and helped PSG win a first domestic treble: his first League Cup victory was followed by a second consecutive French league title, won hands down ahead of Monaco and Lyon, and a Coupe de France win against the third division club Les Herbiers (2–0).

Kylian finished his first season at Paris Saint-Germain with 21 goals, sixteen assists and a second consecutive trophy as the most promising young player in the French league. This was particularly encouraging for a striker playing alongside experienced players like Cavani and Neymar, normally used to leaving mere crumbs for their attacking partners. His new fame also saw the doors of Paris's waxwork museum, the Musée Grévin, open to him. 'I'm proud to be here, surrounded by all these idols, all these people who inspire society, have inspired me and still do,' said Kylian, when his wax double was unveiled on 18 May. Cristiano Ronaldo's statue had taken its place in the museum two years earlier ...

Chapter 19

At King Pelé's right hand

But the season was not quite over. The icing on the cake was still to come … 'All the best players, all the greats will be at the World Cup. It's a chance to show what we can do, our abilities, and there's no better stage than the World Cup for that.'

Kylian was already aware of the challenge that awaited him in Russia when he found himself in the squad of 23 French players called up by Didier Deschamps. His name appeared in the list of strikers alongside Dembélé, Fekir, Giroud, Griezmann, Lemar and Thauvin. There was no Lacazette, no Coman or Martial, and perhaps even more notably, no Karim Benzema.

Kylian's inclusion was not a surprise. Since qualifying against Belarus the October before, he had started in every Les Bleus friendly in 2018 and had played a decisive role every time, with assists against Wales, Germany and Colombia, and even two goals in late March during a 3–1 win against the future tournament hosts in Saint Petersburg.

'He had played his best match against Russia since he was first called up to the side,' said a follower of the France team. 'As well as the two goals he scored, he displayed an incredible sense of calm. The game left its mark in people's minds and led to a funny scene at the exit to the dressing room: while he was answering questions from the press, Olivier Giroud suddenly saw all the cameras turn away from him as the journalists didn't want to miss Mbappé's reaction. Giroud wasn't exactly delighted but what can you do? That's how these things work! Kylian continued imposing himself in the France team in May, with another assist against the Republic of Ireland and a goal against the United States in the final warm-up game before flying to Russia.'

On 16 June, the Paris Saint-Germain striker finally made his acquaintance with the World Cup. At last, he was going to get the chance to experience to the full the competition that had guided him since his earliest footballing experiences on the pitches at AS Bondy. In the first match in Group C, he was confident of his abilities against Australia. He was in the starting eleven in the heat of the Kazan stadium, wearing the number 10 on his back. It was a number he had been given in March, allowing him to add his name to the list of France's greatest players: Michel Platini, in the 1980s, and especially Zinedine Zidane, the hero of an entire country just twenty years ago, when Les Bleus were crowned champions for the first time.

Although they were not considered favourites – unlike Spain, Brazil and the holders, Germany – much was expected of France, provided its young strikers, Ousmane Dembélé and Mbappé in particular, showed up. As early as the second minute, Kylian set off on his first run. His burst of pace down the right wing was followed by a strike that was turned away by the Australian keeper. The World Cup was off to a good start. But it was to be his only chance of the game. Like Les Bleus, who struggled through the gloom to win 2–1, the former Monaco player had been disappointing. He had not been sharp enough in attack and his defensive work had once again left much to be desired.

But he had nevertheless shown enough to stop Deschamps relegating the Paris Saint-Germain star to the bench. Five days later, Kylian was once again included in the France team's starting line-up for their second group game, which was already to be decisive, against a Peru side with their backs to the wall after defeat to Denmark. In the Ekaterinburg Arena, with its huge stand open to the sky, Kylian made his presence felt and wasted no time supporting Benjamin Pavard, just behind him on the right wing. Finally, the unpredictable player who had made a name for himself the previous year at Monaco in the Champions League appeared; with countless little touches and dribbles, which were not all successful but proved his effort, he became part of the game, offering solutions before scoring in the 34th minute. A strike from Giroud was misjudged by the Peruvian goalkeeper as Kylian surged towards the far post and helped the ball into an empty goal. He could surely never have imagined scoring so easily at the World Cup one day. His fifth goal for the national side saw him give France the 1–0 win and, at aged nineteen years and six months, he had become France's youngest ever scorer in the competition. It was better than his compatriots Zidane, Henry and Trezeguet, and not far off other legends such as Michael Owen, Lionel Messi and the king, Pelé, who had set the nets trembling at the age of seventeen in the late 1950s.

But for resounding praise and comparisons with the prodigy of Brazilian football, he would still have to wait awhile. Until 30 June, to be precise. After clinching first place in Group C following a miserable 0–0 draw against Denmark, the French prepared to challenge Lionel Messi and Co, the finalists in Brazil in 2014, who had qualified by the skin of their teeth in Group D behind Croatia. France–Argentina was the pick of the last sixteen ties and Kylian was to make it his own.

But what was going through his mind when he picked up the ball in the thirteenth minute about 30 yards from his own goal, set off on an incredible run, passed two players, left Javier Mascherano standing on the edge of the centre circle and went up a gear in the last 35 yards to get the better this time of Marcos

Rojo, pushing the Argentine defender to foul him in the penalty area? Only the kid from Bondy, the town where anything is possible, could say, although genius cannot be explained. Kylian lets his talent do the talking: as he did in the 64th minute, when he gave France back the advantage at 3–2, placing the ball out of reach of Franco Armani, and again four minutes later, when he sent his team past the Argentines once and for all with an impeccable diagonal shot with the side of his right foot.

After scoring two goals and winning a penalty, Kylian was not only voted man of the match for France–Argentina (4–3), he also became the revelation of the tournament on planet football ... As far as Franco Baresi, a World Cup finalist with Italy in 1994, was concerned, he was 'a phenomenon'. 'Mbappé is like the young Luke Skywalker. You know sooner or later he's going to take over the world. He's a beast!' predicted Alvaro Arbeloa, a world champion with Spain in 2010. 'Said it before, but Kylian Mbappé will be the next global football superstar,' confirmed England's Gary Lineker, Golden Boot winner at the 1986 World Cup, on Twitter. And it did not stop there: the Argentine Jorge Valdano, who had won alongside Maradona in Mexico, forgot his disappointment to praise the young Frenchman in his column for the *Guardian*: 'Mbappé chose the day that Messi and Cristiano Ronaldo left the World Cup to start his revolution. [...] He burst into footballing history, flattening everything before him. From the first minute, he appeared to be made of wind and steel, […] demonstrating a precision at speed that we hadn't seen since Ronaldo, the Brazilian.'

In the move that had led to the penalty converted at the start of the match by Antoine Griezmann, Kylian had been clocked at 37 kilometres/hour. 'Thirty-seven' was also to be his new nickname in the dressing room. But it did not stop there: Kylian became only the second teenager ever to score two goals in a World Cup game. Only the king, Pelé, had achieved such a feat in 1958 in the final against Sweden, and the Brazilian legend took it upon himself to praise the child prodigy: 'Congratulations, @KMbappe. 2 goals in a World Cup so young puts you in great company! Good luck for your other games. Except against Brazil!'

Pelé's wish would be granted. Kylian would not need to test the Canarinha's defence nor subject himself to a brotherly duel to the death with his PSG teammate Neymar. The quarter-final saw France get the better of the tough Uruguayan team (2–0), before seeing off Brazil's conquerors, Belgium, in the semi-final, with another win for Les Bleus (1–0). In these two closed and indecisive games, Kylian was not at his flamboyant best, even picking up a yellow card for an unsportsman-like act against the Belgians. Despite this, he was still valuable for his ability to initiate counter-attacks on the break and bring his technical touch to the ironclad system put in place by Deschamps. A piece of skill from the Parisian against Eden Hazard's Red Devils received widespread admiration: a brilliant back-heel to Olivier Giroud on 10 July in Saint Petersburg. The red carpet was rolled out once again: 'How do you defend against Mbappé?' wondered the former England defender, Rio Ferdinand live on the BBC. 'You look up and say "please help me!"' This moment of inspiration also aroused the admiration of great creative players, such as the Dutchman Patrick Kluivert (winner of the Golden Boot at Euro 2000): 'What movement from Kylian Mbappé! At his age he's showing some incredible qualities at the highest level.' And the living god, Diego Maradona, who said: 'I really like him a lot. For me Mbappé is the revelation of the World Cup.'

Kylian had one last test to pass before everyone would be in agreement: the final at Moscow's Luzhniki Stadium on 15 July 2018. Against Croatia, who had just beaten England (2–1), he appeared serene and determined as the two sides filed out onto the pitch. There was no question of being overwhelmed by emotion during the anthems or destabilised by nerves of any kind. Kylian's dreams and reality had always been easy bedfellows. In the first half, the boy from Bondy had very few touches as he was closely marked by the Croatian defence. Modrić and Co. had understood that the lanky PSG player was France's number one attacking danger. And they were not wrong, as with the few balls that came to him, Kylian seemed capable of making a difference every time. This did not escape Didier Deschamps. Despite being 2–1 up at the break, the French manager urged his team to rely more on its number 10 and to make better use of his calls into space. The effect was immediate.

In the 59th minute, Kylian picked up a deep ball, made it into the penalty area, wrong-footed Ivan Strinić and succeeded at the end of his run in sliding the ball back to Griezmann, who released Paul Pogba. The Manchester United midfielder scored with his left foot on his second attempt. Three–one.

In the 55th minute, Lucas Hernández ran down the wing before crossing to Kylian, who was camped out in the centre of the pitch, about 25 yards from goal. For once, he had time to control it, to look up and check the position of Danijel Subašić and to tuck a right-footed shot just inside the post of his former AS Monaco teammate. The ball bounced once before smashing into the back of the net. Four–one.

In six minutes and just two moves, the Paris striker had put the final out of reach. Lloris's error that resulted in Mandžukić reducing the deficit would not bring the result into doubt (4–2). Twenty years after the generation of Zizou, the French team were crowned World Cup champions again. Kylian finished the tournament with four goals and the trophy for the best young player. At just nineteen, he had achieved the

Holy Grail and fulfilled his childhood dream. On the pitch at the Luzhniki, the boy from Bondy had joined the big time. There was no demonstration of excessive joy but a broad smile and an initial reaction on French television that speaks volumes about him as a person: 'The road was long, but it's been worth it. We're world champions and we're very proud. We wanted to make people happy and that's why we've done all this. I've always said I was in football for the long haul.' And, if possible, so that he can take his place alongside King Pelé, the only other teenager to have ever scored in a World Cup final.

Acknowledgements

We would like to thank the following people for their recollections and collaboration: Benjamin Adler, Atmane Airouche, Éric Assadourian, Markus Bark, Ludovic Batelli, Abdel Belarbi, Oswald Binazon, Gérard Bonneau, Javier Caceres, Souleymane Camara, Irvin Cardona, Alain Caveglia, Damien Chedeville, Timothé Cognat, Jean-Pierre Dardant, Stefan Deppmeyer, Matthias Dersch, Reda Hammache, Margot Dumont, Patrice Girard, Laurent Glaize, Giovanni Grezzi, Yves Invernizzi, Bruno Irlès, Idrisse, Sophie Quéran, Karima, Yann Kitala, David Lasry, Olivier Lombard, Elisa Lukawski, Pierre Michaud, Andy Mitten, Fabien Pigalle, Gérard Prêcheur, Elmire Ricles, Pierrot Ricles, Antonio Riccardi, Guy Rineau, James Robson, Stéphane Roche, Juan-Valentin Romero, Nadine Schaaf, Nicolas Soussan, Jean-François Suner, Théo Suner, Julien Sokol, Sylvine Thomassin, Diego Torres, Guido Vaciago, Javier Villagarcia, Sébastien Vuagnat, Marc Westerloppe and Mamadou Yate.

Thank you to Duncan Heath, Michael Sells, Philip Cotterell, Laura Bennett, Ellen Conlon, Laure Merle d'Aubigné and Roberto Domínguez.

Thanks to Elvira, Céline, Lorenzo, Mathieu, Olmo and Elisa for their support and valuable advice.

Finally, happy reading to Arthur, Jules, Colin, Louis, Tom, Méline and Laure.